Thoughts from the Battlefield

Jean Mallory

Thoughts from the Battlefield

ISBN: 978-1-84961-068-1

RealTime Publishing
Limerick, Ireland

Dedication

To my daughters Tamara, Beverly and Kelly

Children are a gift from the Lord.
...Who are these with thee? And he said, The children
which God hath graciously given thy servant.
Genesis 33:5b

I thank God for giving me the gift of children.

Acknowledgements

With the greatest of appreciation to:

Bernice Riley for her editing suggestions and encouragement,

Rev. T.A. Greene for his support in editing the scriptural content and application,

Dave Hanson and Karen Claghorn for their expertise in editing and helpful suggestions,

Janet Nicolet for her invaluable help, encouragement and mentoring in this writing effort.

CONTENTS

Contents continued;

INTRODUCTION

You might wonder why the title to this writing is 'Thoughts from the Battlefield.' Living in this world is not easy for almost everyone. We all face all the normal hardships and pain that a life can bring. Some might liken this life to living in constant warfare. Financial problems, physical problems along with the strain and pressures of normal living can be difficult to navigate.

It's true, we can have happiness, but we have a lot of pain, heartbreak and sorrow too. Some battles are just skirmishes, easily overcome, and some are devastating, long and intense.

There are different battlefields. There is the battlefield for the soul when we are not saved. You might feel this is a struggle in your inner being, knowing to do right, but not doing it. This extends into the battlefield of the mind, your conscience, or your head knowledge warring against your heart knowledge.

There is a battlefield where Christians grow and mature in the battle, learning, being chastened, and winning victorious battles.

There is a battlefield where those who once knew Christ now wander and struggle aimlessly. Satan fights to keep them from returning to the loving arms of God.

Battles often come to draw us to God or to draw us closer to God. Battles come to strengthen and mature us for that next larger battle that is to come. Battles give us experience to draw on for the future for ourselves or to help others.

Some people think once you become a Christian and begin to live the Christian life that everything is easy. That all our problems are over with and we have nothing else to worry about. In reality, as long as we live in this life, we live in a struggle between good and evil. Satan is the prince of this world and he will fight to keep you from dedicating your heart to the Lord. He doesn't want anyone to commit their lives to Christ and have eternal life.

When you surrender to God and become a Christian, you face continuing struggles. The battles make us more like Him, and soften the clay we are made of, in order for it to be used. Satan would have you to fail and succumb to the world's pressures. He hates to lose anyone to his enemy, Jesus Christ.

The beautiful thing is that if you choose Christ, you don't have to face this battle alone. With Christ on your side and His Word as the supreme guide, you have weapons that cannot fail!

At times, it seems that the battle is too long and the struggle is too difficult, but Christians will win the final battle. The last book of God's Word makes it very clear that Christians win. When you know the outcome of the war, it makes it a lot easier to fight the battles and stand for what is right in the skirmishes.

Christians and non-Christians both have their battles. Perhaps these thoughts will help you to choose which way you would like to fight these battles. Our choice is to fight with Christ or without Him. It makes a big difference in how we fight, and whether we make the right decisions in our own personal battles.

1

THE BATTLEFIELD OF TEMPTATION

OVERCOME BY TEMPTATION

It's just too easy; the bank will never figure out how I jiggled those figures and it still looks like the accounts balance. Now I can go back to the casino and spend all I want. No one will ever know. Patrick's cell phone rang; it was his wife.

"Honey, the pastor called to remind you to be at the meeting tonight about the finance committee."

A stab of guilt hit Patrick for a moment. "Well, I know I headed that committee before, but I just can't handle it this time. Would you call back and tell him I can't make it? Oh, and by the way, would you pack that little bag for me? I have to go on another trip for the bank and be gone for two days."

Patrick broke out in perspiration, knowing exactly what he was doing, and knowing how wrong it was. That gambling problem he had in his younger days was taken care of when he gave his life to God. But now, little by little, Patrick had quit reading the Bible and praying. He stayed away from church more and more. The addiction had returned.

This is the last time, he told himself. *I'll save enough out of the winnings to pay off that big gambling debt and then it's done. I'll turn back to God and no-one will ever know.*

Monday morning, after another weekend of heavy losses, Patrick sat at his desk and knew it wasn't really over at all.

The guilt that had plagued him for months didn't even seem to bother him much today. He thought he could just continue to manipulate the figures, and one day he would get it all straight.

Two men that Patrick did not recognize walked over to his desk and one spoke. "Mr. Trent, we are bank examiners and we've been here all weekend." He continued firmly, "Could we see you in the manager's office please?"

Galations 5:1 Stand fast therefore in the liberty wherewith Christ hath made us free, and be not entangled again with the yoke of bondage.

~~~~~~~

Christians are made in the likeness of Jesus and are expected to do whatever Christ has called them to do. Christ has freed them from the bondage and entanglements of the world to perfect them in His work.

Paul wrote that they can become entangled again with the yoke of bondage if they are not careful to stay close to him and abide by His teachings.

Satan will use any weakness a person has to ensnare them again and pull them away from what is right. It's up to each individual to "stand fast and not be entangled again" by staying close to Him and continuing to do what they know to do.

****

TEMPTING GOD

Ken ran out the door and jumped into his car. The car roared out the drive and onto the curvy rural lane. He thought, *I just can't be late again for work. I'll lose that job for sure.*

He knew he shouldn't drive fast on that narrow dirt road. It was lined with trees that dropped off into the deep swamp in several spots. *Just this time, he thought, I won't drive this fast again.*

The sharp curve to the left was coming up quickly but Ken knew he had made that curve before going almost this fast. *Oh no, there's a car coming, I'll have to swerve right.*

Ken panicked as he felt the car careening through the brush and down the slope to the swampy waters. When it settled, he realized he wasn't hurt badly. He managed to pull himself out through the window since the door was jammed. He was so glad the swamp waters were low and not flooded, as he made his way up the steep bank.

In his mind he heard his Dad's words, '*You know this car is a deadly weapon; it can kill you and others. Be sure and treat it as such.*'

The other driver had stopped to make sure Ken was okay, and told him that he would call for a wrecker. "I can't imagine how you missed all those big trees and came out without being hurt." He shook his head wonderingly, "God's hand was on you for sure."

His parents felt the same way. "You know God has protected you several different times, but you still refuse to turn your life over to Him," his Dad said that evening. "What if you hadn't made it out of there? Where would your place in eternity be right now?"

Ken knew his Dad was right and he seriously thought about making a change in his life. Gradually as time went by, he forgot the fear of that day.

He turned back to his fast-paced life and lost the desire to make any changes in his way of life. Maybe someday he would, when he was older and more settled down. He was young and could just take his chances until then.

1 Chronicles 28:9 And thou, Solomon my son, know thou the God of thy father, and serve him with a perfect heart and with a willing mind: for the LORD searcheth all hearts, and understandeth all the imaginations of the thoughts: if thou seek him, he will be found of thee; but if thou forsake him, he will cast thee off for ever.

It's easy to feel like we have plenty of time to make a decision or a change, but... what if we don't? The timetable of this world is not in our hands, but in the hands of the one who made it.

Every day, unexpected things happen that could easily hurt us or claim our lives no matter what our age or situation. Often, people put off becoming a Christian because they think it's a dull life with no more fun or happiness. On the contrary! The Christian life is a life of unspeakable joy and peace. Just ask someone who lives that life.

****

TEMPTED TO RUN

Benny swallowed hard, trying to get past the lump in his throat. It was his first mission in the Mideast. The Master Sergeant outlined the attack and did not spare the details of what had happened to the mission just before theirs. Their amphibious assault vehicle had been hit by a roadside bomb. None of them made it out alive.

As they received their instructions, the ambulances arrived again and began to unload those who were severely hurt and in pain and those who were unconscious. Marines who were previously alert and strong just a few hours ago were now suffering. Now his squad would be the one to try and complete the mission. Benny, just out of high school, had been so anxious to join the Marines.

Benny really didn't understand what it meant to be on the battlefield, until this first deployment. Now he knew. The temperature was above 120 degrees. Danger lurked everywhere; sand seeped into everything. Wounded troops were constantly being brought in and the Marines suffered more than their share of casualties.

Fear gripped Benny's mind. For just a moment, he thought, *I'll pretend to be sick, go to the infirmary. I'll tell them I'm too sick to go on the mission.* It was only a moment.

Then his mind immediately went to the training he had received, the pride, and the Marine motto - 'Semper Fidelis.' Yes, always faithful. It meant set apart, a group separate and different, unlike any others. 'Semper fi' meant a tremendous amount to this young Marine. It was Latin, the language of the law. It meant faithful **always**, not **sometimes**, not **usually** and not **when the conditions are just right**.

Ashamed of that fleeting thought that came to his mind, pride rose up in him. A Marine is always faithful to his mission and faithful to each other. He would stand and be faithful. Whatever the outcome, he was here to serve, to fulfill his mission.

1 Corinthians 10:13 There hath no temptation taken you but such as is common to man: but God is faithful, who will not suffer you to be tempted above that ye are able; but will with the temptation also make a way to escape, that ye may be able to bear it.

1 Corinthians 4:2 Moreover it is required in stewards, that a man be found faithful.

~~~~~~

We send armies to fight battles. But armies are made up of divisions, squadrons, platoons, squads and individuals. Each person must respond personally and be ready to complete whatever mission they are assigned to. If each person is faithful, then the army is faithful overall.

Faithfulness includes obedience as a normal way of life. It expresses itself in extreme loyalty, even when it means self-sacrifice and giving.

Temptations can be overcome, if your mind is on being obedient to your strong training. This life requires each and every one to be faithful to whatever task they are assigned.

Soldiers have to face the unknown in every battle. They can turn their backs and run, or stand and fight with courage.

Christians also have a choice to wallow in self pity in the battles or to keep fighting and believe God in the midst of the battle the way David did.

1 Chronicles 28:20 And David said to Solomon his son, Be strong and of good courage, and do it: fear not, nor be dismayed: for the LORD God, even my God, will be with thee; he will not fail thee, nor forsake thee, until thou hast finished all the work for the service of the house of the LORD.

****

TEMPTED TO GIVE UP

*W*hat next? Avery thought, *first the lung problems, now the doctor says there is definitely permanent liver damage. Not much hope at all. I wish that guy in the bed next to me wouldn't be so cheerful; after all he has a terminal illness, too. I am so tempted just to give up and end it all. What do I have to look forward to anyway? I could just save up these pills, and take them all at once.*

Jeff in the bed next to Avery, closed his Bible and pondered on the scripture he had just read. *Wow, that is a really good thought.* He had been reading in Mark 14 where the disciples were told to follow a man carrying a pot of water to find where their Passover meal would be held.

Mark 14:13 And he sendeth forth two of his disciples, and saith unto them, Go ye into the city, and there shall meet you a man bearing a pitcher of water: follow him.

Mark pondered about how Christians are also told to follow a man with water, the 'living water' of eternal life. He wondered if that might be a good opening to share with Avery. Avery needed Christ in his life so badly.

"Hey, Avery, I want to talk to you about something."

After a while of listening to his roommate, Avery responded, "Are you saying I could ask Jesus to come into my life and everything would be OK again? Do you mean I wouldn't be sick? If that's true, why hasn't your cancer gone away?   I think I've just about decided to terminate this miserable life. It couldn't be any worse to be dead, could it?"

"Well, Avery, God does heal diseased bodies sometimes, but other times he doesn't for His own reasons.

You know when we leave this life, our lives don't really end. We make a choice while we're living in this life as to where we'll go.

If we repent, we'll spend eternity in Heaven. That's a place without any disease, hurt or suffering. The Bible says that those who die without repenting will suffer eternal torment in the lake of fire.

It's important to know that everything doesn't end when this life ends. We will still live forever, somewhere! God promises us eternal life in heaven if we accept Him, instead of eternal torment in hell."

~~~~~~~

People contemplating suicide must realize they are just trading an earthly battlefield for an eternal one.

It's not true that Christians are perfectly healthy and free of any hindrances or diseases. Just because people get saved, doesn't mean their bodies are free from the consequences of the sinful life they previously lived. Heavy drinking, smoking and drugs all cause disease and problems in their physical bodies.

People also suffer disease even if they have lived healthy strong lives. God is God and He is supreme. He does heal bodies, but not always. It's enough for Christians to know that if they stay close to Him, they will be with Him in heaven.

Christians often fight through disease, or whatever personal battlefields they must go through. It's enough to know that Christ gives them a calm and joyful spirit to endure to the end through all of these things.

****

ADDICTED

It all began so innocently. Just a little pop-up window on the computer that Mitch clicked on by mistake and then he naively began to look at the different sites that all promoted pornography.

At first, Mitch told himself that he needed to be aware of things like this because of his teen-age boys, but slowly he realized the truth.

The attraction began years ago and he had always fought it. He tried to limit himself to the glossy magazines which he kept hidden. Now he knew it was much worse than he had thought. He couldn't stop, he truly was addicted.

He kept the different computer sites secret and always tried to log on to them when he knew he would have privacy. One day Dianne walked in on him unexpectedly. If he couldn't break this habit now, he knew it would end his marriage.

It was something he couldn't resist, even at work. Twice, he almost got caught by someone when he was using his work computer to watch those compelling videos.

Mitch had always prided himself on his strength to resist and stop bad habits, like smoking. But this was something he now realized he could not control by himself at all. Desperately, he walked into the church office for his meeting with the pastor.

Ephesians 5:3-5 But fornication, and all uncleanness, or covetousness, let it not be once named among you, as becometh saints;
Neither filthiness, nor foolish talking, nor jesting, which are not convenient: but rather giving of thanks.

For this ye know, that no whoremonger, nor unclean person, nor covetous man, who is an idolater, hath any inheritance in the kingdom of Christ and of God.

~~~~~~~

Deliverance begins with repentance. Mitch has to understand there was something within himself that was not right from the beginning or he would have never given in to the addiction in the first place.

A weakness or a perverse will fosters lust. Giving in to that lust turns into habit. Habits when not resisted turn into necessities.

Mitch was bound by his addiction. Complete repentance and cleansing would free him from that.

Luke 6:18,19   And they that were vexed with unclean spirits: and they were healed.
And the whole multitude sought to touch him: for there went virtue out of him, and healed them all.

Healing and deliverance from addictions is still available today.

****

2

THE BATTLEFIELD OF DISTRACTIONS

PRESSURES OF LIFE

"Sorry mom, the bus is coming I don't have time to take out the trash now." Colby hollered as he ran out the door. "I'll get it earlier next time."

"Hi, Colby, did you get that history project finished?" his friend asked when he sat down beside him.

"Oh no," Colby groaned, "I had to practice for the band concert and finish the book report. Then Dad wanted me to mow. I guess I shouldn't have slept so late Saturday. I probably shouldn't have gone to the ball game Saturday night either. I can't seem to keep up with anything anymore."

"Don't forget, you promised to speak at the youth meeting tonight."

Colby shook his head sadly. There just isn't enough time, and I know my priorities aren't right. I'll have to call and let them get someone else.

~~~~~~~

Ezra 7:6 This Ezra went up from Babylon; and he was a ready scribe in the law of Moses, which the LORD God of Israel had given: and the king granted him all his request, according to the hand of the LORD his God upon him.

Ezra was a *'ready'* scribe. Verse 10 of that chapter tells how he had prepared his heart to seek the will of the Lord and to do it. He was ready to do whatever was needed. It takes organization and preparation in our busy lives to be ready.

It's necessary to pray and study and put in the hours, usually giving up some things that can be relinquished. The pressures have to be put in the right perspective. Organization is a must. It takes time to learn the priorities and try and put 'first things first'.

There are years of elementary school and high school before one reaches college. There can be years of applying ourselves in study and prayer before God can use us. We prepare one day at a time and the preparation must continue if God is to continue to use us.

John 9:4 I must work the works of him that sent me, while it is day: the night cometh, when no man can work.

****

NOISE

Ezekiel 13:2 Son of man, prophesy against the prophets of Israel that prophesy, and say thou unto them that prophesy out of their own hearts, Hear ye the word of the LORD;

Pastor James pulled into his driveway. The talk radio program was loudly giving their views on the current situation. He grabbed his briefcase, full of materials and the bag of reference books, hoping to glean enough information to complete the outline needed for Sunday's message.

Exiting the car, one of his board members called his cell phone and expounded his view of the problem they were having in the church.

"Hi, honey. I just got home a few minutes ago myself," spoke his wife from the living room.

"I've spent the entire afternoon listening to the administrator tell us why we have to vote on building the new wing. Let me share his opinions and tell me what you think." She followed him towards his office.

"Kaylee, please turn that stereo down," James called loudly above the noise as he walked toward the hall. The twins were glued to the blaring television in the family room, not even noticing that their parents were home.

James dropped the briefcase and bag on the desk in the office, while trying to listen to his wife's report on her work situation.

The telephone loudly interrupted and Mrs. Bennett demanded that James immediately settle a family discussion about what the visiting evangelist preached on Wednesday night.

~~~~~~

Instead of listening and being distracted by all the noise around us, we must first go to God, the source of our strength and ask Him for His guidance. Then we must hear what God tells us in His Word. There are too many distracting things to hear, to read, to comprehend and listen to in this loud world. We've forgotten what quiet and silence is.

Many voices speak and sometimes we try and discern the importance. We make decisions based on the world's input instead of God's direction.

Each source seems to have its own slant on what we should absorb and believe. Their views so often come from corrupt and inaccurate worldly wisdom.

God speaks truth to us from His Word. True wisdom and guidance comes when we read, hear, study and meditate on the Word of the Lord.

1Kings 19:12 And after the earthquake a fire; but the LORD was not in the fire: and after the fire a still small voice.

****

INFLUENCES

"But, Mom, I've just got to have this outfit. It's the same exact style like Cali Davis wears. Don't you understand? All the girls dress like she does. I've got to dress in that style, too."

"No, honey, you really don't. You spend far too much time watching that TV show, and you're beginning to act more and more like Cali Davis, instead of Madison Carter. Your school work is showing a lack of attention, too. Let's put Cali Davis on a once-per-week basis and bring you back to reality a little bit."

"I guess you're right, Mom, but it's all my friends ever talk about. I sure don't want to be an outcast and not be able to talk to my friends about what Cali is doing," Madison answered.

"Madison, why don't you join the youth band at the church? It will give you something else to concentrate on and you love playing your flute. Maybe your friends would like to become active in the youth group."

"Mom, that's a really good idea. They said they needed more players in the band. I guess if I give up the Cali Davis show, I'll have plenty of time to go to the practices."

~~~~~~~~

Philippians 4:8 Finally, brethren, whatsoever things are true, whatsoever things are honest, whatsoever things are just, whatsoever things are pure, whatsoever things are lovely, whatsoever things are of good report; if there be any virtue, and if there be any praise, think on these things.

Thoughts from the Battlefield

We tend to become what we partake of. What we surround ourselves with influences our lives. If we watch the things in the world, listen to the popular worldly influences and play with the things in the world, we will become like the world in our thoughts and desires. If our mind is stayed on Godly things, we will be more like Him.

****

CONTINUING

"I seem to be swamped with responsibilities lately. I just can't teach that class any longer. I've taught for twenty-two years now. I'm sorry, but I think it's time that someone else took a turn preparing a lesson every week and facing the unruly six-year-olds. I'm just really tired and I need a break, Mr. Willis." Linda turned to walk out of the superintendent's office.

"Could you just continue on until I can find someone else to step into your place? Perhaps teaching just a week or two?" Mr. Willis pleaded.

"Well, I'll try. But you've got to find someone soon," she answered. "The difficulties are getting to me. There must be someone that has more time than I do. The pressures at work are just about unbearable."

~~~~~~

Daniel 1:21 And Daniel continued even unto the first year of king Cyrus.

What an example for us in our trials. For seventy years in captivity in a heathen land, Daniel 'continued'. We cannot even imagine the hindrances and temptations he must have faced. Yet he continued to do what was right.

Getting thrown in the lions' den because of his worship, didn't hinder him. We have choices in our lives to live, work and worship where we want to. Daniel was under control of heathen leaders.

We sometimes want to be diplomatic and politically correct in what we say, but Daniel spoke the truth to the leaders he served under.

It's true we can become overburdened with our responsibilities, but sometimes just putting them into the right perspective and organizing differently can help.

Most of all, if we turn everything over to the Lord and ask for His help, the way Daniel always did, most things will just fall into place.

Daniel never had to endure captivity by himself. He always could rely on God to be right there with him helping and guiding every step of the way.

****

SO TIRED

"Honey, you know you fell asleep in church again tonight. This is really unusual for you. You've always been bouncing with energy from 5:00 am to midnight. I want you to see Dr. King this week. Maybe you just need vitamins or something." Kaden sounded concerned.

Lisa yawned her reply, "Sure, Kaden. I'll try and get that in, maybe Friday noon if they can see me."

"Dr. King, I just don't know what is wrong with me. I'm so exhausted all the time. Not just in my body, but I'm having a hard time focusing mentally too. I can't begin to keep up with all the demands on my time. My muscles ache and no matter how tired I am, I have a hard time sleeping."

"Well, Lisa, the tests results look OK, but tell me about your average week and what you do every day."

Lisa grabbed her date book from her purse. "Let me see. You know I work by appointment. I have a lot of time for other things. I probably have around 15 appointments a week. Then the activities of the children take time, like transportation to school, music and band. Soccer games and practices are usually on Thursday and Fridays. I coach those too.

Tuesday nights I volunteer at the nursing home. Wednesday night I help with the church programs and Sunday I take care of the Children's Church program.

We also have the normal doctor and dental appointments. I was elected head of the PTA this year and we meet on Mondays. Because of Kaden's position, we need to entertain at least once a week and have several guests for dinner.

Oh yes, I also take care of my Dad and transport him to places. I try and keep his housekeeping up as well."

Dr King shook his head, "That's enough, Lisa. Tell me when you rest and do something for yourself?"

"Hmmm, well I don't really rest, except at night. There is just always so much to take care of."

"Your problem Lisa is exhaustion! You are wearing yourself completely out. These bodies were never meant to go non-stop without some rest.

I want you to cut out at least a third of your activities and don't fill that time in with any added responsibilities. Learn to read, take naps, and start an enjoyable hobby. You must get some rest or your body will give out entirely," Dr. King warned sternly.

~~~~~~~

Genesis 2:2 And on the seventh day God ended his work which he had made; and he rested on the seventh day from all his work which he had made.

God in His wisdom, created the earth in 6 days. He then created a day of rest. Rest is necessary to recover strength, refresh our minds and spend some time in quiet prayer and worship. God didn't get tired of working; He simply completed the work of creating the earth. God doesn't get tired, but man does and the human body needs rest.

When Jesus came to this earth in the form of a man, His body also needed rest.

John 4:6 Now Jacob's well was there. Jesus therefore, being wearied with his journey, sat thus on the well: and it was about the sixth hour.

Of course this stop was part of God's plan to minister to the woman of Samaria, but His body did need rest. He also slept when He needed to recover His strength in His human form.

We often forget to take the time for the rest and recovery our bodies need. This world is entirely too busy! Satan would use these many distractions to not only wear out these bodies, but also keep us too busy to have fellowship with the One who created us.

It's important to try and continue in God's work and whatever ministries He has given us to do. Often, we find we are overloaded with worldly hindrances that drain our time and energies. Those distractions can be cut back or eliminated.

Hebrews 4:9-11 There remaineth therefore a rest to the people of God.
For he that is entered into his rest, he also hath ceased from his own works, as God did from his.
Let us labour therefore to enter into that rest, lest any man fall after the same example of unbelief.

The rest for a Christian is not only rest from physical work, but it is a spiritual rest and refreshing.

****

3

THE BATTLEFIELD OF INDIFFERENCE

LUKEWARM

"What makes you think your church is so great anyway?" Deanne questioned. "I'm a Christian too. There's got to be other good churches. It's not that important to be so particular, is it?

I like just visiting around and never getting too involved. I learn a lot about other churches. It's fun and entertaining. I don't think it's necessary to go to church so much anyway. It's enough for me to go just once a week or so. If you go more than that, especially if you go just to one church, they might ask you to get involved. You know, like join a committee or something."

Laurie silently prayed before she answered her friend. "I do think my church is the best around here. Why would I want to go to a church that wasn't the best when we have a choice and freedom of religion? My church teaches and preaches the truth of God based upon the Word of God, the Bible. The doctrines are true, accurate and Bible-based.

A church isn't a social hall where we go to be entertained. It's where we go to learn about God and assemble together with others that believe as we do. We hear messages there that help us to grow as Christians and correct us when we get on the wrong path. We have altars there where we can pray for ourselves and others that need prayer. Many of us do 'help out' by teaching, singing, ushering, praying or whatever needs to be done in the church family. We do it gladly and joyfully.

Another important thing," Laurie went on, "is my church family. When I have a crisis, they call, send cards, pray, bring food or whatever is needed. This is the family that I will be with forever in Heaven as long as we all stay true to Christ.

I love God with all my heart and I want to learn about Him. I want to work for Him and most of all be prepared to go to Heaven when He calls me home. Being faithful in my church helps me to do this."

Deanna answered, "But aren't there a lot of hypocrites in churches, just pretending to be what they're not? You don't want to get involved with them, do you?"

"Aren't there hypocrites everywhere?" asked Laurie. At least in church they just might get saved and change. I'd rather go to a good church that might have a few hypocrites, than to avoid church and maybe not make it to Heaven."

~~~~~~~

Revelation 3:16 So then because thou art lukewarm, and neither cold nor hot, I will spue thee out of my mouth.

Spiritual Lukewarmness is a sad state to be in! If Deanne is saved, she is a lukewarm Christian.

Coldness can be remedied. Anyone can come to God and be saved. To be on fire spiritually is when you can be used for God, to work for Him and tell others of the gospel message.

Being lukewarm is so pitiful. Just enough spiritual warmth and head knowledge to sort of be considered a Christian, but too cold to work for God, to share the gospel or to be of any use in Christian work.

Lukewarm is on the verge of reverting to coldness. It's on the verge of warming up to be useful but settled in a mushy, stale spot and not useful at all.

****

WORKS

"Janie, I just don't understand it. We always go to church, sometimes twice a week, even inviting other people to go with us sometimes." James paced the floor speaking loudly.

"I work in the church, too. Oh I don't teach or anything, but when they need donations, I'm the first to contribute to whatever fund it is. I think I always write the biggest check. I always volunteer to go on the work-days and help with the physical labor, too. We always give our 10% tithe, down to the penny.

We help missions and other charities whenever anyone needs help. Remember my picture was in the paper last week giving that big check to charity?

I'm the one that should have gotten the seat on the deacon board, not Charlie. I know we do more for the church than Charlie does. Don't you agree? We've been in that church a long time.

You've always worked in the church, Janie, and given your time to the hospital committee, too. We've donated lots of money to that." James stopped and sighed. "Maybe we should just take our money and time someplace else where it's appreciated."

~~~~~~~

James and Janie really don't understand the meaning of salvation. They think if they work hard enough, they will be accepted and earn a high place in Heaven.

They're not working in the church because they love Jesus and want to do everything they can do for Him. They're working to earn position and the approval of man.

Jesus said we are saved by His grace and not by what we do. He gave His life for our salvation. He didn't say we needed to work for His approval.

Thoughts from the Battlefield

Ephesians 2:8, 9 For by grace are ye saved through faith; and that not of yourselves: it is the gift of God: Not of works, lest any man should boast.

****

APATHY

Wendy sadly drove by the darkened church. It used to be so vibrant, so alive with many cars in the parking lot. A friend of hers had attended there. Now they still had a Sunday morning service but that was all. For a while, they rented it to another church on Sunday nights and Wednesday nights; now it was dark with no life at all this Wednesday evening.

Her friend said that after a big conflict, when quite a few people had left, fewer and fewer came at night until it was only two or three. Even those few got so discouraged with the dull services that they went elsewhere, too.

The people that were left didn't care much for the new leadership. There was no one to play the piano or lead the singing. No one wanted to help or teach and all the programs ended. That's when it seemed there was no life in the church. Other things became more important to the people than going to church.

The people still came to church on Sunday mornings; it was more out of habit than anything else. There was nothing to encourage them to have evening services. There was no desire to learn or worship. Everyone felt they received all they needed on Sunday mornings.

Song of Solomon 2:15 Take us the foxes, the little foxes, that spoil the vines: for our vines have tender grapes.

~~~~~~~

It's the little things that come in one by one, which enter into our lives and cause apathy to take hold. To be apathetic is to be deprived of passion, without feeling, indifferent, unconcerned. It can happen to anyone and sometimes they never recover and pull themselves out of their apathetic condition.

It's very sad when churches die because of the little things. There is a way out. When you think certain things have ended in your life and no longer interest you, follow the example of Paul and Timothy.

2 Corinthians 1:8,9 For we would not, brethren, have you ignorant of our trouble which came to us in Asia, that we were pressed out of measure, above strength, insomuch that we despaired even of life: But we had the sentence of death in ourselves, that we should not trust in ourselves, but in God which raiseth the dead:

Paul and Timothy stopped trusting in their own selves and trusted even harder in God. It's a mistake to let apathy or despair overpower you or even influence you. The answer is to trust God. Press in with all your strength and let Him lead you. Sometimes churches will fall, but don't be the cause of it falling and don't fall with it.

****

I DON'T NEED TO REPENT

"Honestly, Mom, I don't see why you make such a big thing out of this. You know what a good person I've always been.

Ever since you and Dad went to that new church and 'got saved', you've been pushing me to go and do the same. I really think God looks at our lives and sees that we don't steal, kill or hurt anyone. He knows that we are good people.

Now you want me to go to the altar and 'repent?' What should I repent of? I've always been the good child. Remember? I help others, I work hard and I always did well in school, too.

I never tell lies or cheat or anything bad. I'm just a good person. There isn't any need of becoming a fanatic, is there?

God knows I've got a good heart and I'm a good person. Some people were just made good and we'll go to Heaven too!"

His mom thought a minute and then answered, "Let me remind you of something that happened a long time ago, Cole. You were about 3 or 4 and had just learned to write your name. Your brother was a year younger and just loved to scribble. You were both coloring with crayons in a book and I went in the other room for a minute.

When I returned, there across my white walls, written in a red crayon were the letters C-O-L-E. Almost speechless at what I was seeing, I automatically asked the question 'Who did that?'

Of course I knew your little brother couldn't even write his own name, let alone yours.

Immediately you pointed to Larry and said, 'he did'. Now you were just a little boy, far too young to understand the meaning of salvation, but that sin nature is built into each and every one of us.

A small child tries to protect himself instinctively against punishment by lying. Lying is wrong and it is a sin. A good nature isn't built into anyone. But the instinctive evil nature is.

One of the first words a little child learns is 'No!' That is the normal disobedient nature that is part of all of us from the beginning of life."

Ephesians 2:3 Among whom also we all had our conversation in times past in the lusts of our flesh, fulfilling the desires of the flesh and of the mind; and were by nature the children of wrath, even as others.

"Of course as you grew, we taught you not to lie or steal and to be a good moral person, but that isn't enough for salvation. We are all sinners. Some are saved because Jesus paid the penalty for sin when He died on the cross for us. All we have to do is believe that, repent of our sins and ask Jesus to come into our hearts."

Romans 3:23 For all have sinned, and come short of the glory of God;
John 3:3 Jesus answered and said unto him, Verily, verily, I say unto thee, Except a man be born again, he cannot see the kingdom of God.
Matthew 3:2 And saying, Repent ye: for the kingdom of heaven is at hand.

~~~~~~~~

Some people think they are really good enough to make it into Heaven on their own. They just don't think of themselves as sinners. But it is very true that all have sinned and there is only one way to enter into the joy and glory of Heaven. And that is by repentance.

Repentance leads to the new birth in Christ. It is the means Christ uses to re-create and transform our lives. We might be 'good' by the world's standards, but apart from Christ, all people by their inherent nature are sinners.

Psalm 51:5 Behold, I was shapen in iniquity; and in sin did my mother conceive me.

****

ONE-SIDED RELIGION

"I'll let you know from the beginning. If you have any religious views, just keep them to yourself. I don't want to hear it and I don't want religion crammed down my throat." Christy spoke very firmly to the hospice lady.

Connie answered quietly, "I'm here to help and take care of your husband. I know you've been through a very hard time in the last few months. We can talk about anything you want to. You seem to have had a rough time in the past concerning religion. I'm sorry."

Tears filled Christy's eyes as she thought of the past. "My mom and my sister used to shake their fingers in my face and tell me I was going to burn in hellfire. I was always so scared, because I didn't know what that meant. I don't even speak to my sister anymore because she won't stop preaching."

Connie nodded as she answered, "It seems like some people are just extra zealous because they don't want to see their loved ones die and miss going to heaven. It's not always the best way to reach people."

"It's really sad," she went on, "because right now you are under such a heavy burden and I hate to see you carry it alone."

"What do you mean?" Christy answered. "Who else is there? I don't have anyone but myself."

Connie silently prayed for help before she answered. "Christy, what you've heard, are all the negative things about what could happen if you don't accept Christ. You've never heard about all the wonderful benefits Christians have. Would you like me to tell you about some of them?"

~~~~~~~

Sometimes overly zealous Christians can do a lot more harm than good if they just present Christianity as one-sided. They want to push everyone into getting saved by scaring them. Getting saved to avoid eternal condemnation is certainly a good motivation, but the entire picture must be presented as well.

Revelation 3:20 Behold, I stand at the door, and knock: if any man hear my voice, and open the door, I will come in to him, and will sup with him, and he with me.

Jesus drew people to Himself with love and compassion for their burdens. He wanted to help them. He said I stand at the door and knock. He didn't shove the door down and browbeat them. He knocked politely and said, if you heard His voice and opened that door, He would come in.

We must never forget that refusing Him does have consequences, but we must understand that the Christian experience is full of joy and happiness as we rely on His loving care and compassion.

****

4

THE BATTLEFIELD OF
SELF-RELIANCE

BUILDING FOR ETERNITY

"Wow, you made the dean's list again, Jackie. What are you going to do after graduation?" asked her friend Pat.

"I intend to continue on towards getting a master's degree, while I start my own business in computer science. With some luck and lots of hard work, I intend to make my first million by the time I'm 30. That's all it takes, you know. Just determination, study and hard work," Jackie confidently answered.

"I'm going to the revival tonight at our church. Why don't you go with me?" questioned Pat.

"Oh no," Jackie answered, "I sure don't have time for that stuff. It's just a waste of time. I need to research the best city to start my business, and complete a paper for extra credit."

~~~~~~

Ezekiel 13:14 So will I break down the wall that ye have daubed with untempered morter, and bring it down to the ground, so that the foundation thereof shall be discovered, and it shall fall, and ye shall be consumed in the midst thereof: and ye shall know that I am the LORD.

Jackie doesn't realize she is in a battlefield - the battlefield of self reliance. Hard work can be a good thing, as long as we put God first! Setting goals, building a business, getting good grades are all good achievements when God is the solid foundation that these things are built upon.

Throughout history, mankind has been convinced that his destiny was in his own hands, and that man was capable of astounding accomplishments. The Titanic was heralded as the greatest ship ever built and completely unsinkable because of the superior design of man. This proved to be unfortunately wrong for hundreds of people.

What is the foundation of our lives? What is the substance that foundation is built upon? What elements are we using to hold it all together? Perhaps we're using our wits, our talent, or our educational qualifications. In the end, all will be found lacking.

Anything completely man-made without Christ can be compared to untempered or unhardened mortar. Mortar that has not been strengthened will fall. It is not strong enough to stand on its own for long. It might stand for a while, but it will never make it to eternity. It will be found unstable.

God's strength is needed in every endeavor to be lasting. His strength is the element that hardens the mortar. Man is not in control of destiny, God is. The only true foundation for our lives that will never fail us is Jesus Christ.

****

SHEEP

A small boy in Palestine was learning about tending sheep in the fields. He listened carefully and watched because he wanted to be a good shepherd like his dad.

"Why do the sheep need so much care? Why can't we just let them graze on their own, the way we do other animals? What would happen?" The small boy asked.

"Joseph, without the shepherd, the sheep wouldn't have a chance of survival," he answered. "Sheep are very dumb animals; they would graze and eat all the grass in an area and then just starve because they had no-one to lead them to fresh pastures. They can't find water on their own, so they would probably die of thirst. They'd get lost and tangled up in the briars and if they rolled over on their backs, most of the time they can't turn back over by themselves."

"They love and trust their shepherd, Joseph. He always goes in front of them to lead and guide them to the best pastures, the fresh water, and to keep them from any danger from wild beasts. He never goes behind them to drive them. A loving shepherd leads the way."

"But look Dad, that man is behind his sheep and he is driving them. Why isn't he leading them instead?" Joseph pointed in the distance to a man with a group of sheep.

"That man is not a shepherd, Joseph. He is a butcher and he is driving the sheep to the butchering area to be slaughtered."

John 10:27,28 My sheep hear my voice, and I know them, and they follow me:
And I give unto them eternal life; and they shall never perish, neither shall any man pluck them out of my hand

~~~~~~~

We, like sheep, also need a shepherd to lead us through this life. Many are the hindrances and battlefields we will face. It is so much easier to face them having one to lead and guide us.

Our shepherd loves and cares for us so much that He gave His life for us.

John 10:11 I am the good shepherd: the good shepherd giveth his life for the sheep.

It is so comforting to know there is one that loves us so much that He actually died for us. How could we not follow Him and trust Him to keep us and lead us out of danger?

Why would we want to be reliant upon ourselves when He is there with open arms just waiting for us to completely surrender our lives to His care? He's the one who knows the safest route to follow. When we face those trials that make us strong and help us to grow, He's always there to help and comfort us.

He gently leads. He does not drive. It's necessary to hear and follow Him, but He'll never force anyone to turn to Him. Free to choose? Yes, always, but do we really want to go on our own?

****

BITTERNESS

"Can't I call your son for you, Carl? You know there's not a lot of time left," gently spoke the doctor.

"No! No! He's tried to come or call me so many times over the years, but I've never been able to forgive him. I worked so hard to put him through all those years of school. I knew he would be a great attorney.

Then he threw it all away to become of all things the pastor of that little church. I wanted him to take over the practice, but it just disintegrated when my partner died and I had to quit working, too.

I've never understood and it's tormented me all these years, how he could have really made something of himself and he gave it all up."

"Is there anyone else I can call, Carl?"

"I don't know who. I've never given anyone else the chance to hurt me the way he did. After Sue died, I just stayed alone."

"Hi, Mr. Reese, I'm Pastor Parker. The doctor asked if I would step in here for a minute. I just wondered if anyone has ever told you how you can be free from the bitterness that has been with you for so long."

~~~~~~~~

Psalms 51:10 Create in me a clean heart, O God; and renew a right spirit within me.

Bitterness is a destructive, corrosive element in a person's life. It's like a speck of rust on metal and if left alone, it will eat and grow until the metal is consumed and weakened.

Like rust, bitterness in a person can grow until it is all consuming and nothing else matters. It leaves a strong person weak and twisted in their mind.

Things don't always go the way we planned in our lives or the lives of our loved ones. Although we may sometimes be hurt, we can't give in to the bitter, unforgiving spirit that would eat away at our soul.

Jesus can take away pain and disappointment that life can bring. Leaving the joy and peace behind that only He can bring.

******

SELF-SUFFICIENT

It was August 1945. The little girl didn't really understand what it was all about, but she sat near the fence on the lawn and waved her flag like all the other people were doing. They kept saying, 'It's finally over. Now they're coming home.' But her daddy didn't come home.

Her sisters took care of her since her mom had to work two or three jobs just to get by. At night her mom worked at the telephone office in that tiny town, and they let her mom sleep on a cot between the few calls that came in. That way she usually got enough sleep so she could clean houses or pick fruit on the farms in the daytime hours. She made enough to make ends meet for her family.

They rarely went to church but occasionally attended the big church that was near, when they did go. When she was five, her mom and sisters decided she needed to be baptized. So the next Sunday morning, they gave her a push to go down the aisle when the invitation was given.

What she remembered most about the baptism was the pretty blue blouse her sisters made for her. All of her clothes were hand-me-downs and this was brand new, just for her.

Often, Della was pretty much on her own since her sisters worked part-time and kept busy with their own affairs. She learned to be very self-sufficient.

They moved around several times and when they were in a neighboring state, one sister got married. The other two followed before Della was 10. She learned to rely on herself more and more. Her mom always encouraged her to be independent and take care of things by herself.

Occasionally, they attended a church, but they usually didn't live anywhere very long because her mom constantly looked for better work opportunities. So they never really got involved in any church. Della looked at church as just kind of a social thing to do once in a while.

Her mom remarried when she was 14 and Della didn't get along with her step dad. He was abusive and looked down on all women. As usual, Della just relied on herself and stayed away from him. Her confidence in her own abilities increased.

Della married young, mainly to get away from home, but it wasn't a happy marriage. Determined to make it work, she tried very hard but after 16 years and two children, she began to realize that she couldn't fix everything. It ended when he left her for someone else.

Several years later, while working in a small store and struggling to support her children, she realized one certain man kept coming in the store daily and was showing an interest in her.

He was different from most of the other people she had met in her lifetime. Older, more mature, but it was more than that. He had something she had rarely seen in her self-dependent life. He had a personal relationship with God. They dated and married after a few months.

Now, several years later, she was facing the most traumatic situation of her entire life, the terminal illness of her dearest companion. She knew she could not handle this. It was way more than her capabilities. She had always believed she could handle anything and was completely self sufficient, but now it was impossible. She couldn't face the possibility of losing her husband. She was so tired of trying to take care of this herself.

This totally helpless feeling made her realize that she wanted to have that close relationship with God that her husband had. She had watched so many others go through rough times but only those that truly knew Christ had the personal strength needed to endure.

Della knew, regardless of the outcome, of this certain situation, she had to have that dependence on God and not on herself. With a broken heart and spirit, she sank down on her knees to ask forgiveness and committed her life to Jesus.

~~~~~~

Matthew 11:28, 29 Come unto me, all ye that labour and are heavy laden, and I will give you rest.
Take my yoke upon you, and learn of me; for I am meek and lowly in heart: and ye shall find rest unto your souls.

Many people are not privileged to grow up in a Christian home and they are not encouraged to live for Christ. Instead, they are taught to depend on their own strength and capabilities. Self-sufficient people face the same situations life brings to all people, but there is a difference in how they handle hard times.

Christians know they can't handle everything. Indeed, there is hardly anything they can handle by themselves. But we know the one who can take care of everything in a much better way than we can. His solutions are always perfect, unlike the solutions of man.

Emerging from trials as a Christian leaves one stronger and able to help others after the trial is over. Recognizing the supremacy of God and the inadequacy of man is the first step on the way to living a fulfilled life.

****

CHANGED

"Well, Stan, I know I need to get saved. I'm tired of trying to do this on my own and messing things up so badly. I really think I'm ready to commit, but… there's just one thing that bothers me."

"What is that, Clay?"

"Well, you just spend so much time in church. I don't want to *have* to do that. Sunday is the only day I can take the boat out or do what I want to do. All the Christians I know spend a lot of time in church. Is it a requirement or something?"

"Clay, the Bible does say not to forsake the assembling together of ourselves. But more than that, the church is a place where we grow and mature as Christians. There are many that cannot attend church. They might be bedridden, or in hospitals, or even just live too far away to attend.

In some countries, Christians are a minority and the churches are very few. God knows all about our situations and He loves us individually where we are. If it's not possible to go, then God will help us right where we are.

But if we have the opportunity to worship in the house of God and we don't, we can grow cold and drift away from Christ.

You see Clay, when you get saved, you will have the desire to worship and learn more about Him. The church helps us to learn and become more like Christ. The church family is also very supportive and helps us through the rough times. Many are closer to their church families than they are to their natural families."

Hebrews 10:25 Not forsaking the assembling of ourselves together, as the manner of some is; but exhorting one another: and so much the more, as ye see the day approaching.

~~~~~~~~

What Clay really didn't understand was that when someone is saved and commits their life to Christ, they are changed! A wonderful change takes place, and the things that a person once thought were so important, are not so important after all.

Their values completely change and they see things as they really are, in light of eternal values. It's hard to explain until you have experienced it, but *changed* is the perfect word. Christians are a new creation and all things are made new.

II Corinthians 3:18 But we all, with open face beholding as in a glass the glory of the Lord, are changed into the same image from glory to glory, even as by the Spirit of the Lord.

****

5

THE BATTLEFIELD OF DECEPTION

ONE WILL BOW

"I just don't know what to do, Pastor. What is your advice? I really don't want this new group to influence those that are serious about learning. Shall I ask them to leave? Or do you think the study will help them to learn?

They seem so confident but they just aren't quite sincere and devoted in their beliefs. Now, my original ladies are becoming attached to them and adapting some of their mannerisms. It's hard to tell which ones are sincere and which ones aren't."

Shelly taught a morning Bible study each week. Recently, a group of ladies had joined in, but their lifestyles and values were lacking compared to the original group. Now they were affecting the lives of the others in that they really didn't take the Bible study seriously.

Pastor Martin knew the group Shelley was speaking about. He thoughtfully said, "Let's see what Jesus had to say about this situation."

Matthew 13:28-30 He said unto them, An enemy hath done this. The servants said unto him, Wilt thou then that we go and gather them up?
But he said, Nay; lest while ye gather up the tares, ye root up also the wheat with them.
Let both grow together until the harvest: and in the time of harvest I will say to the reapers, Gather ye together first the tares, and bind them in bundles to burn them: but gather the wheat into my barn.

"They seem sincere but not really devoted like the others. How will the tares be known in the harvest?" asked Shelley.

"Well Shelley, actually it will be quite easy. When the wheat sheaves are ready for the harvest, the heads are heavy and they will bow. The tares will stand straight up and refuse to bow," smiled Pastor Martin. "Those that truly worship Christ will have a different spirit. The Word says they will be known by their fruit. They will prefer others to themselves and their spirit will be humble. Those that are not really committed will have a proud, arrogant spirit. It will be very obvious."

~~~~~~~

Many resemble Christians in what they say and do. But, how many actually are Christians? Have you ever felt like someone just was not quite truthful in the way they tried to portray themselves?

Only those who recognize Jesus as the Lord of all will make it into Heaven. Only those who humbly realize His holiness and recognize their own unworthiness have the true spirit of Christianity.

****

IT SOUNDS GOOD

"Hi, Callie, I think I found an answer to the problem of where to have the wedding and I also found a nice group of people to be with," Cliff began when she answered the door.

"Well, tell me what you've found," Callie answered as they sat down in the living room.

"There is a new group meeting in that old church on Elm Street. You know the one that just closed down last year. It's like a church, but not a church. They are kind of like me, you know, they don't really believe in joining a church or anything. But they wanted to have a group where they could gather and get to know each other."

"They'll provide a nice place to get married or even hold a funeral if necessary. They have ethical talks and self-help groups that will meet on a casual basis, when it's convenient for everyone. It's a social group with no pressures or obligations to follow any kind of guidelines. What do you think?"

Callie chewed on her lower lip, "Well, it does really sound good but, Cliff, I've been thinking a lot about whether there really is something about believing in God and going to a real church. What if Aunt Molly is right and there is a God, and a real heaven and a real hell? For some reason, this group just kind of worries me. It's a church but not a church?"

Mark 13:5,6 And Jesus answering them began to say, Take heed lest any man deceive you:
For many shall come in my name, saying, I am Christ; and shall deceive many.

Thoughts from the Battlefield

Many are deceived in our time. Atheist groups, social groups and so-called churches are growing and becoming popular. They sometimes look innocent and good, but actually they have a much darker message. Satan, the angel of death, is promoted in such groups, although this is disguised as self- promotion.

Social groups and atheism have never saved, healed or set anyone free. God, and only God, can do these things. Conforming to a social group to meet one's needs is a big mistake. Jesus is the only one who has the key to eternal life.

****

BONDAGE

Brad listened dejectedly as the judge read the sentence. Oh, boy, he was really in trouble this time. First rehab, then court-ordered testing, parole, places that he couldn't go, curfews, and so many other requirements that had to be fulfilled.

Well, at least they didn't sentence him to any of those Christian programs. After all, those people are so bound up; they can't do anything that's fun. He didn't want anything to do with that restrictive life.

Brad loved what he thought was his freedom; he depended on alcohol and sometimes drugs, to get that completely free feeling.

Yes, it did get expensive and he had to depend on illegal means to support his fun habits. Of course that led to stealing from his family and other things. But Brad really loved running his own life the way he wanted to.

This rehab and all the other restrictions didn't sound like a lot of fun. He had been in trouble before, but this time he had gone too far. It didn't sound like he would have any freedom for a long time.

Isaiah 5:20, 21 Woe unto them that call evil good, And good evil; that put darkness for light, and light for darkness; that put bitter for sweet, and sweet for bitter! Woe unto them that are wise in their own eyes, and prudent in their own sight!

~~~~~~~

Brad thought he was free, but he was completely tied up by his lifestyle. He was bound by drug and alcohol addictions and not free at all.

He thought that Christians were bound up and lived a restrictive lifestyle, but it was really the total opposite.

Christians are completely free and live a blessed life. They are free from addictions. Any restrictions in their lives are there because they choose to live a life that is pleasing to God. It is their choice, not by bondage.

Brad's happiness in his way of life is completely temporary. There's no happiness in constantly searching for your next drink or trying to find drugs or money to further the search.

The Christian lives in a place of safety, knowing that he is kept and protected by the Lord. When a person does not live in the presence of God, he is exposed on all sides to worldly dangers that can easily destroy him.

Psalms 91:1, 2 He that dwelleth in the secret place of the most High shall abide under the shadow of the Almighty. I will say of the LORD, He is my refuge and my fortress: my God; in him will I trust.

****

CHALLENGING THE WORD

It was a great family barbeque. The entire family rarely had a chance to get together and they really had a wonderful time visiting and catching up on everything.

"Well, it's been a lot of fun, everyone, but I've got to get to the house and get some studying in," said Dave.

"Are you still teaching the class in that church?" asked Fred.

"Yes, why don't you all come and visit sometime since you're not attending any other church?"

"Oh, come on now, Dave, you don't really believe that stuff in the Bible, do you now? All that stuff like walking on the water, and the virgin birth and even the parting of the sea. You know that can't really be true, don't you?"

"Well, Fred, I know the Bible is true for several reasons. One reason is that reading the Bible transforms lives. Many become saved and their lives are forever changed.

The Bible is full of prophecy that has accurately been fulfilled and is still being fulfilled.

The unity of the Bible also tells me that it is true. It was written by at least 40 different authors in 66 different books, but they all agree and go together as one unit.

The Bible has existed for many years. It was written over a period of approximately 1,600 years, some parts are over 4,000 years old, yet it's still applicable and still accurate.

No other writing shows such quality, depth and perception.

The Bible is accurate. It has been proven over and over in history, by records, by scrolls, the Rosetta stone and many other proofs.

Most of all, I know the Bible is true because of its power. Nothing else can pierce hearts and minds and lead people to salvation, healing of their bodies, and other life-changing events.

You know, Fred, it's really very clear. Unmistakable truth, backed up by historical facts. Why don't you read it and then decide if it's true or not? Dave questioned."

~~~~~~~

Isaiah 55:11 So shall my word be that goeth forth out of my mouth: it shall not return unto me void, but it shall accomplish that which I please, and it shall prosper in the thing whereto I sent it.

All truth, no matter how clear it is in the scripture, will be challenged in this dark world. Christians should be ready to defend God's Word and state the reasons why the Word of God is accurate.

****

DECEIVED

"You can't be serious, Brent! Everyone knows that my lifestyle is accepted nowadays. Science has just about proven that we were just born this way. That's what determines whether we're gay or not.

You're my own brother, surely you don't hate me the way those other fanatics do," shouted Art hotly.

"I don't hate you at all," answered Brent. "I hate that sinful lifestyle that you're living. Just like Jesus loves the sinner, but hates the sin, I love you very much. You've bought into a lie, Art, and now you are completely deceived."

"You're wrong! You're trying to deprive me of my sexual freedom. I go to church, too. We have a church that just preaches the love of God and how everything in the Bible isn't real clear on some things like gay lifestyle."

~~~~~~~

Leviticus 18:22 Thou shalt not lie with mankind, as with womankind: it is abomination.

There are no grey areas in Biblical truth. The sin of homosexuality is detestable to God. He placed within each person a pure sexual drive, only meant to be used within the bounds of marriage between a man and a woman. Outside of that, it would be impure, unholy and ungodly.

Homosexuality is not new. Genesis 19 speaks of the cities of Sodom and Gomorrah. These cities were throughly depraved and consumed with this sin. "Sodom" is where we derive the word 'sodomy'. God destroyed these cities so completely that He removed the evidence that they ever existed. The sites have never been found.

Thoughts from the Battlefield

Leviticus 20:13 If a man also lie with mankind, as he lieth with a woman, both of them have committed an abomination: they shall surely be put to death; their blood shall be upon them.

1 Corinthians 6:9 Know ye not that the unrighteous shall not inherit the kingdom of God? Be not deceived: neither fornicators, nor idolaters, nor adulterers, nor effeminate, nor abusers of themselves with mankind...

See also *1Timothy 1:8-10, Romans 1:27*

****

JUST READ AND BELIEVE

"Hi, Chelsea, did you ever recover from that bad infection on your leg?" Lois spoke into the phone.

"Actually it seems worse this week. I'm supposed to go to the wound care place this afternoon and see if they can help me. I think the worst is this awful depression that presses into my mind. I can't seem to shake it off," answered Chelsea.

"I'm so sorry, Chelsea. Let me tell you what I do when I'm really down about something. Now don't laugh, I'm not one of those fanatics or anything. What I do is to read the book of Psalms. Sometimes I read for a couple of hours or so. It just always seems to help.

Now, I don't go to church or anything like that and I haven't changed my lifestyle at all. But just reading that book and believing that it will help really does. I get away by myself and sort of pray while I'm reading. I don't do it every day, of course, but when I have a problem and really believe it will help, it always comforts me."

Mark 1:15 And saying, The time is fulfilled, and the kingdom of God is at hand: <u>repent ye, and believe</u> the gospel.

~~~~~~~

The book of Psalms is a great book, and it can be very comforting. Our faith however, should be placed in God and not just reading one book of the Bible.

The verse above stresses repenting and believing, and not just believing. You can't separate repenting and believing, or true faith will not happen.

Repenting and believing results in the conversion of our soul. That's when we place our faith in God and He comes into our life. It then changes our lives. We are truly different.

No longer do we want to live a sinful lifestyle. No longer do we avoid church and the things of God. There is a love for others within us. There is also a peace in our hearts that replaces any turmoil and strife.

****

6

THE BATTLEFIELD OF DISCONTENTMENT

A PURPOSE

"No, I didn't get that job at the new bank or the one at the mill. I went by the church too. Bill said he didn't need me now but he would call me if he needed another teacher.

The car broke down on the way home. I couldn't fix it so I had to have them tow it to the garage. Sometimes I really feel like a failure. Anything I try to accomplish, I fail at." Allen sighed as he entered the kitchen where his wife was cooking dinner.

"Don't worry, honey, and don't be defeated. God knows where you are and He has something wonderful for you to do, if you just stay ready to be used. We've got to keep our trust in God, even in the rough times and even when we can't see what is ahead. We know He does have a plan for our lives."

~~~~~~

Jeremiah 1:5 Before I formed thee in the belly I knew thee; and before thou camest forth out of the womb I sanctified thee, and I ordained thee a prophet unto the nations.

God does know each and every one of our situations. We might not be called to be a prophet like Jeremiah, but we are called to be and do something.

There is a purpose and a plan for every life. Satan would lie to us and tell us, "You have no purpose. You're not important and you have no abilities. There is no plan for your life." These are total lies with no truth in them!

We might not all be called into full-time ministry, but all have a personal calling. God makes the plan and He never makes a mistake.

Thoughts from the Battlefield

There is no one like you. If we look at science, no one is created with the same DNA or the same fingerprints. God didn't use a cookie cutter when creating us. All are created to be exactly what He intended us to be. He made us who we are and when He is ready and at the perfect time, He will reveal His purpose for our lives.

****

IT'S MINE

"No, I will not give up the house!" Jimmy shouted loudly. "You can have the summer house in the mountains, but I'm not losing this place. I've worked hard to make these payments and I want it!"

Susan fiercely answered, "You know my family is near, and it's close to everything. You're the one that wants the divorce. I get to keep the house. I want my car and the summer place, too. These things are really important to me. You're the one who cheated, not me."

"Well, they're important to me, too, and I'm not going to keep making the payments for you to live here," Jimmy retorted.

Susan replied, "I thought maybe you would like an apartment in town close to the children's school and they could stay with you, but I really need to have these other things. I've decorated this entire house and I'm going to keep it."

~~~~~~~

The battlefield of an unhappy marriage is a sad situation, idolizing material things to the extent that marriage and children are no longer important at all. This world with its mindset of "things" is having a tragic effect on lives. If we're not careful, all of us tend to have idols. Idols can be anything from people to tangible or intangible things.

What do you idolize? Perhaps it is your accomplishments in life, your position, your home, your job, children, husband or wife. Perhaps your idol is entertainment, - like TV, movies, vacations. While "things" might have a place in our lives, we can't idolize them. Only God is to be worshiped and idolized. All else will crumble, disintegrate, fade away or perhaps change and grow away from us.

Ezekiel 14:6 Therefore say unto the house of Israel, Thus saith the Lord GOD; Repent, and turn yourselves from your idols; and turn away your faces from all your abominations.

****

THE TROUBLEMAKER

"I just don't understand," Gabriel spoke to his mom dejectedly. "Why does Dad favor Mark so much, when he is just so mean? He's always gotten in so much trouble; we didn't even know where he was for two years.

Dad has spent a fortune searching for him and paying his bills. Now, just because he's decided to turn over a new leaf, Dad is bending over backward to welcome him back home. I've never been in trouble like Mark, but I don't ever remember Dad making such a fuss over me."

"Oh, Gabriel, you know your dad and I love you just as much as Mark and we do so much appreciate what a good, faithful son you have always been. It's just that when one child is lost and not saved, the situation consumes a parent's heart until that lost one returns home. Then the relief is so great, the parents want to celebrate.

We've always loved and supported you and did everything we could for you. But it's like your brother was dead to us ---- lost and in trouble. Now he's repented and come home. All of these years, we've rejoiced with you, appreciated you, and we've celebrated your faithfulness.

Now we're condensing all those empty years when Mark was gone into one big celebration for his repentance."

~~~~~~

Luke 15:4-6 What man of you, having an hundred sheep, if he lose one of them, doth not leave the ninety and nine in the wilderness, and go after that which is lost, until he find it?

And when he hath found it, he layeth it on his shoulders, rejoicing.

And when he cometh home, he calleth together his friends and neighbours, saying unto them, Rejoice with me; for I have found my sheep which was lost.

A little further down in that same chapter of Luke, it tells the story of the prodigal son. It tells of his brother who became angry at the attention the prodigal received.

Some things are hard to understand until you become a parent yourself and have the same situation with one of your children. There certainly is no intent to slight one over the other. But when one repents and comes back home, it is certainly cause for rejoicing.

Luke 15:31-32 And he said unto him, Son, thou art ever with me, and all that I have is thine.
It was meet that we should make merry, and be glad: for this thy brother was dead, and is alive again; and was lost, and is found.

****

EMPTINESS

The reporter scribbled quickly then asked, "Mr. Dempsey, Just what is it that brings you the most happiness in your life?"

"Hmm... happiness, I'm not real sure I've found happiness yet. I enjoy a lot of things like traveling and seeing new things, but I guess I've just about seen it all now.

I collect expensive racecars and homes and enjoy trying to find more. I always thought that just one more big purchase or one more house would be what I really wanted, but it never was enough," he answered.

"All that money and you're not really sure you've found happiness? What about your beautiful children? You've been married several times, right?"

"That's true," Mr. Dempsey answered, "exactly six times, but the children all preferred to live with their mothers and my wives just wanted money. You see, Tom, I now realize that there is an empty place inside of every man and they can search their entire lives to fill it, but nothing seems to bring that peace and fill that place.

I have a friend who is a Christian and he says that when he got saved, the empty place was filled with peace. I wonder now if he is right, because I've tried everything else. I guess it's too late now to try and make things right. I doubt there is a place for me anywhere."

~~~~~~

Mr. Dempsey is correct about the only way to fill that empty place in one's heart, but he is wrong about it being too late. Only if you die without Christ, is it too late. As long as you are alive and can ask Him into your heart, it's not too late.

Revelation 3:17 Because thou sayest, I am rich, and increased with goods, and have need of nothing; and knowest not that thou art wretched, and miserable, and poor, and blind, and naked:

Satan's mentality, as well as the world's is to become rich with tangible goods. That's the world's view of happiness… wealth, just a round of expensive pleasures and purchases. But in reality, riches only make us spiritually poor and blind.

Satan uses "wealth" to create a false security; a false security to make us think that we don't need God. We only need a new job, a bigger house, more clothes, or a nicer car. But these things will never satisfy when we're hungry for spiritual riches.

****

THEORY OR FACT

James had wondered how Mr. Kensington, the science teacher, would handle this subject of creation. Now he realized it was much worse than he thought.

"Now, surely you all understand that this world did indeed come about by a huge explosion in the universe. I just cannot understand why anyone would believe in some kind of creator with some design and purpose."

Mr. Kensington ignored the several raised hands in the room. "Now, we won't have any discussion about this subject. This is the most accepted theory and it's the one we'll talk about in this class."

James dejectedly stared at his homework pages. "I just don't understand, Mom. He is so determined that he is right. It's enough to make me question my own beliefs. He won't even let anyone else question him.

Is there any way that an explosion could have happened to make the earth? I don't like that science class. How can I spend the rest of the semester in there?"

"Well, Honey, I understand how difficult it is. Let's look at some scripture to reinforce what we know is true. First of all we know the Bible is absolute truth, right? It has been proven so many times, in so many ways."

At James' nod, she went on. "***Genesis 1:1*** **says: *In the beginning God created the heaven and the earth.*** We know that evolution is a theory and not a fact. We know that the Bible is true and we can't believe both the truth and a theory.

This world had a real specific beginning. Truth always agrees with the Word because the Word has been proven to be true."

Thoughts from the Battlefield

Psalms 14:1   To the chief Musician, A Psalm of David. The fool hath said in his heart, There is no God……..

Those who have empty hearts have said, 'there is no God.' It reflects their emptiness. If they can erase God, then they can erase their own accountability to a higher power. But if they refuse to believe and worship God, they will worship something.

They will worship self. They can deny God all day long, but they can't change the fact that God is real.

Christians have to live in this world, even with all its lies and denial of God. They have to live here and live with all the adversity until they go to Heaven.

Christians are in the minority, yet they need to firmly stand on what they believe and not be swayed.

****

7

THE BATTLEFIELD OF DEATH

AN END AND A BEGINNING

Despair gripped Blake as the agony of an approaching loss consumed him. He watched the hospice nurse as she examined Jill.

Turning to him, she said, "Not much longer, now."

"She won't suffer, will she?" Blake had witnessed death many times in combat, but this was so personal, his dearest mate of 50 years.

"I can give her morphine, if you want," she replied.

Knowing that she was serene and content, so far, and how pain-free she seemed, he replied, "That probably won't be necessary." The nurse left and said she would return soon.

Jill opened her eyes and weakly said, "Remember, Honey, the only sting of death is sin. This will only be a light affliction, only for a moment.

I'm just going to sleep and transition from one place to another. Please try and be comforted, knowing that I'm in the presence of the Lord and you will join me before long." Jill patted his hand, and Blake felt an amazing peace fill the room. She looked at him one last time with a smile of joy on her face.

~~~~~~~

2 Corinthians 4:17 For our light affliction, which is but for a moment, worketh for us a far more exceeding and eternal weight of glory.
Psalms 116:15 Precious in the sight of the LORD is the death of his saints.

When Christians die, they enter into peace and glory. It is precious to the Lord to receive them home. It is the end of their lives here on earth, but it is certainly a glorious beginning to their lives in Heaven.

God gives dying grace to the Christian and takes away the fear. There is no fear, because there is no sting when a Christian dies. Instead it is a passing from one place to another and the heavenly home is incomparable to anything in this life.

Luke 16:22 tells us the saints are carried away by the angels. What a comforting thought. They are gently and carefully gathered up and carried home.

Paul tells us in *Philippians 1:23*, how much better it is to be with Christ than to stay here.

Of course we grieve when that loved one dies, but a study of God's Word will remind us that we can go to them and be with them again in that glorious heavenly home.

****

NO MAIL TODAY

"Oh, Clint, she's only been gone two weeks, and I miss her so much. I think I miss her the most when I get the mail and there's nothing from her. She was always so good to write long newsy letters, or even just a card, but she always sent something every few days," lamented Lillie.

"I know, Sis, I never realized how much I enjoyed her letters. It seems letter writing is a lost art in this day. She always sent a note or a card at least once a week. Now the box is full of bills and junk mail."

Clint went on, "I guess we need to concentrate on what is really important. Our sister is in that heavenly home and no longer suffering.

Perhaps we need to remember we have the most important letter of all and thank God for His letter to His people. It doesn't come in the mailbox. It's always here, just waiting for us to pick it up and read. It's old, yet so new, always that fresh wonderful Word, full of history, good news and guidance."

Psalms 119:105 Thy word is a lamp unto my feet, and a light unto my path.

"You know, Lillie, I remember a time when I didn't really understand that letter from God. But now that I'm a Christian, most of it is crystal clear. We know some of it will be revealed later. It's good to look forward to the time when the rest of it will be shown to us."

1 Corinthians 13:12 For now we see through a glass, darkly; but then face to face: now I know in part; but then shall I know even as also I am known.

~~~~~~

Yes, we miss very much the things associated with the loved ones that have died.

It's very true that God can fill that empty place left in our lives. His Word is of utmost importance for everyone. It's always on time and always seems to apply to whatever situation we are in.

It leads us, guides us and answers our questions. No matter how many times we read it; it always seems fresh and new and applicable to our needs. It's a holy, precious, personal gift to each one of His children.

Reading God's Word is vital to anyone. It holds the keys to daily living, fighting battles, healing and living in this world. Most of all, it holds the key to eternal life, salvation.

Praying is when we talk to God. Reading His Word is one way He speaks to us.

****

WITHOUT HOPE

"That's what he said Mom. The doctor said that nothing they can do will work for long and to call in the family," Dawn sobbed into the phone. "He said there wasn't really any hope that he would even leave the hospital."

"Oh, Honey, I'm so sorry. I'll take care of calling everyone. But please remember, with God there is always hope and I'll be praying."

Praying! Dawn didn't even know how to start praying. Her husband was a Christian but Dawn relied on herself. Never had she felt so hopeless and alone. She hung up the phone in the waiting room and sunk down into a chair. The tears were still rolling unstoppable down her face. She didn't even notice the sweet-faced lady across the room move towards her.

"I noticed you're having a difficult time," she said. "Would you mind it I prayed for you and your loved one who is in intensive care?"

Pray.... there was that word again! "Well, I... I guess it's OK," Dawn answered in a small voice. "It's my husband, he's only 46 and they don't think he'll live."

The lady put her arm around Dawn and in a soft voice, prayed for a miracle and for God to touch Dawn with strength. She asked God to help her to be reliant on Him.

She spoke to Dawn a while about how there is always hope in God and how He can give us the strength to face anything.

Psalm 42:5 Why art thou cast down, O my soul? and why art thou disquieted in me? hope thou in God: for I shall yet praise him for the help of his countenance.

Dawn realized the prayer helped her to have a small measure of peace in her spirit and she thanked the lady.

Many hours later, after the family had arrived, there was no change in her husband's condition. He seemed to be a little more stable but the doctors still did not give them any long-term hope.

The family urged Dawn to go to the hotel room they had rented and get a little rest. She had not left the hospital for several days. It was close by and they could call her if needed. She didn't want to leave but thought a shower would be helpful, and agreed to leave for a short while.

Dawn sat in her hotel room chair for a moment before returning to the hospital. She just couldn't keep from crying. She was full of fear for what the future would bring.

She noticed the Gideon Bible on the table and opened it, wishing she could find some peace. Her mind was filled with the torment of possibly losing her husband. The scripture seemed to jump off the page at her.

1 John 4:18 There is no fear in love; but perfect love casteth out fear: because fear hath torment. He that feareth is not made perfect in love.

She realized that perfect love was found only in Christ and that perfect love would give her the peace necessary to go on.

Kneeling, Dawn knew she must commit her life completely to Christ. She had recognized the peaceful countenances of those who had Christ in their lives and she knew she wanted that perfect love in her own life.

Regardless of the outcome of her husband's illness, she knew she needed to be a child of God to face whatever would come. She asked God for forgiveness for her sins, and asked Him to please come into her life.

Dawn's husband pulled through that crisis and lived eleven more years despite the disabling heart condition that was a part of his life. They learned to live every day fully and appreciate his extended time on this earth.

Thoughts from the Battlefield

Dawn learned to stay very close to God. She loved God's Word and read and studied it every day. She praised God for extending her husband's life and for giving her a new life in Christ. In the darkest time of her life, she found God and realized she was no longer alone.

****

GUILT

The call came about mid-morning, informing Brock of his dad's death. He thought about how little he knew his dad. It had probably been 10 years since he had gone back east to visit his family.

Brock's earliest memories were of running with his brothers to get the sheriff to lock up his dad because he was drunk and beating up his mom, again. They divorced when Brock was about 5 and they moved to another state.

The contact between them was almost non-existent. Brock sent an occasional card, and his dad wrote sometimes. They visited a few times but the distance and lack of any real connection made it difficult. He rarely even thought about him.

Now, as the day wore on, Brock was tormented with the fact that he had never made any attempt to witness to his dad or tell him about Christ.

Unable to sleep that night, he walked the floor, prayed and read the scripture. The guilt was very strong and he felt he should have tried harder to develop some kind of relationship.

Part of a scripture floated in his mind and finally he looked it up as he felt God was trying to speak to him. He found the scripture in *Isaiah 55:8.*

Isaiah 55:8 For my thoughts are not your thoughts, neither are your ways my ways, saith the LORD.

Brock felt peace in his heart as he read these words. He felt that the Lord didn't hold him responsible for his neglect. However, Brock vowed to try harder in the future to share the Christian message with others as the Lord would lead him.

Several days later, after the funeral, Brock spoke to his aunt who had been faithful to visit his dad daily at the nursing home. She related to Brock how his dad had visited the chapel the day before he died. He stayed a long time. When he returned, he told her that he had made his peace with God. Brock rejoiced that his dad was now in heaven.

~~~~~~~

We are responsible as Christians for spreading the gospel message. But God understands our situations also and there are times when distance or other circumstances separate people. God also knows when it's the right time to reach someone. If we push the message upon them without God's leading, it could drive someone further from the Lord.

If God wishes you to witness to someone, He will lay that person on your heart and give you a burden. You will know what is expected of you if you stay close to God. Remember Satan will torment the minds of Christians any chance he gets.

****

THE CHILD

"I think I always knew it was wrong. But since I've been saved, I know it was wrong and the thought of what I did, keeps tormenting me.

When reading the Bible, I keep finding scriptures like the one in *Jeremiah 1:4, 5.* It says God knew us and formed us while we were still in the womb," sobbed Courtney.

"Yes, Courtney," replied Rebecca Slater, "It's very true. God breathes life into a child at the moment of conception. You were deceived into thinking otherwise and the pressure from your boyfriend and your parents must have been devastating."

"I should have been stronger. How can God ever forgive me for that? How can I ever forgive myself? I consented to destroy the life of a precious, innocent child; *my* precious child." Courtney continued to sob in the arms of her Sunday school teacher.

"Courtney, God forgave you the moment you repented at the altar and He not only forgave you, but he has forgotten your sins and wiped the slate clean."

1John 1:9 If we confess our sins, he is faithful and just to forgive us our sins, and to cleanse us from all unrighteousness.

Psalm 103:12, says: *our transgressions have been removed from us as far as the east is from the west.*

"Let's look for a moment and someone who was the cause of many to be murdered. Remember the story of Paul. He was called Saul when Stephen was stoned and *Acts 8:1* says *he was consenting to his death."*

"Do you think Paul might have been tormented about those Christian deaths after he was saved?"

"Yes, he must have been," answered Courtney.

"Courtney, God can take anything and use it to make us into what He wants us to be. Let's look at what Paul said a little further along into his ministry.
In *Acts 17:28* he said, ***For in him we live, and move, and have our being...***

You see Courtney, to forgive ourselves total dependence is required. If our eyes are completely on the one who saved us, then the guilt of the past is removed. That sweet little child is in Heaven right now and God has forgiven you and will not remember it again."

Hebrews 10:17   And their sins and iniquities will I remember no more.

"We also have to be sure that we have forgiven all the others involved." Her teacher continued.

Matthew 6:14, 15 For if ye forgive men their trespasses, your heavenly Father will also forgive you:
But if ye forgive not men their trespasses, neither will your Father forgive your trespasses.

"Then, depend on God to give you the peace in your heart and enable you to help and minister to others, perhaps young girls that are in the same situation that you faced."

****

8

THE BATTLEFIELD OF DESPERATION

ONE TOUCH

Lily was truly desperate. She knew she couldn't go on much longer. People shunned her, hated her and were afraid of her. She was so alone. She had been sick for so long. Every cent of her parents' money and her own had gone to the physicians.

What torment they had put her through. She went through the pain, the suffering, but it was all to no avail. Now she was even worse. She still had the issue of blood. Everyone knew what the Word said.

Leviticus 15:2 Speak unto the children of Israel, and say unto them, When any man hath a running issue out of his flesh, because of his issue he is unclean.

Twelve years without being able to touch anything or anyone. Twelve years… unclean. She was so weak and frail, what little strength she had was about gone.

Perhaps the one they call the Master could heal me as He has healed others. But.... how? The crowds are so thick. I can't touch anyone. How could He even know that I was near Him? I'm too weak to call out and make myself heard. Maybe if I could just touch His robe.

The crowd was so thick; she could blend in without anyone noticing her. The border of the robe trailed to the side of the narrow street where so many pressed in and followed Him.

There, I can just reach it. "Oh" she cried aloud with tears flowing down her face, *I'm healed! The issue of blood has stopped, my strength has come back. I can feel the color return to my face.*

"Who touched me? Jesus asked." He knew and now she must confess.

Trembling, she answered, "It was I, dear Master. Please forgive me. I meant no harm, but I knew you could heal my body."

Luke 8:48 And he said unto her, Daughter, be of good comfort: thy faith hath made thee whole; go in peace.

~~~~~~~

Daughter!! How beautiful that He recognized her as one of His own. She had been cut off from her people for years. She was not allowed to go near other people, including worshiping in the synagogue. But now He recognized her as His child. Yes, she was a daughter, with a childlike faith to believe for healing after years of pain and abuse.

He responded to her faith by performing a miracle. A touch was all that was needed, and she was instantly healed.

Sometimes when we have no place else to go, and our situation calls for desperate means, all we have to do is turn to the Master. He will respond when we reach out to touch Him.

Although this story was taken from the true story that happened about 28AD, it's still true today. Jesus heals our bodies when we reach out with our prayers to touch Him. *Hebrews 4:15* tells us He cares about our infirmities.

****

WHEN THE CLAY CRUMBLES

As the steel door clanged shut behind Monica, she had never felt so alone in her life. She pondered on what brought her here. It was just a little pot, just a few pills, I just needed a little cash that day and I had some extra pills. Who would have ever known that woman was an undercover policewoman.

That worldly hardness came into her mind briefly *I'll just be smarter next time,* she determined. But then the awful reality of the situation hit her, "No, no, it's over, I know it's over, and there will never be a next time." The hot tears rolled down her face and she sobbed uncontrollably.

"Hi, feel like talking?" a voice on one of the bunks asked. For the first time, Monica realized she was not alone in the cell. As her sobs diminished she moved away from the barred door and sat down on the other bunk.

"No, I don't want to talk right now," Monica answered.

"I've been there and I really understand," said the other woman, "There's an extra Bible on that stand, and I find that's what helps most of all."

"Yes, maybe that's what I need right now. That's what I've needed for a long time. Thank you," replied Monica, and the tears began again as she opened God's Word.

~~~~~~~

Jeremiah 18:4 And the vessel that he made of clay was marred in the hand of the potter: so he made it again another vessel, as seemed good to the potter to make it.

Thoughts from the Battlefield

Jeremiah 18:6 O house of Israel, cannot I do with you as this potter? saith the LORD. Behold, as the clay is in the potter's hand, so are ye in mine hand, O house of Israel.

All people were made by God to be used as vessels for His purposes. The strength of a vessel depends on the condition of the clay. The clay can be contaminated with things that are not of God. The clay can be weak, depending too much on its own strength. It can be flawed, disintegrating with too many of the wrong elements to be useful.

A clay pot that is no good can be broken and remade by the potter. Christians can also be crushed and broken by the one who made us. He then reforms us. We come out of the process stronger, purified and in much better condition after the trial which crushed us.

Monica was crushed by her circumstances. In that desperate time, she turned to the master potter to learn and be molded again by the one who created her.

****

STANDING ALONE

Stewart leaned against the concrete of the overpass. He had joined the ranks of the homeless. First he lost his job, and then after the unemployment ran out, he lost his apartment too. Without family or any close friends, he now was on the brink of despair.

He had prayed, but seemingly God didn't answer. He wished he had gotten more involved in a church or made more friends, but it was all too late now. Hot tears fell from his eyes and again he began to pray.

"Hey, Stewart, is that you? It's Joe Woods from the community church. You visited us a couple of times. You told me you were a good carpenter. I've been looking for you for days now. But I just couldn't track you down after your job ended."

~~~~~~~~

Daniel 10:12 Then said he unto me, Fear not, Daniel: for from the first day that thou didst set thine heart to understand, and to chasten thyself before thy God, thy words were heard, and I am come for thy words.

Often we stand alone without human help to face extended battles. We pray, but there seems to be no answer. We feel we are facing the battle completely alone. God knows what we are going through and has heard our prayer from the beginning. Daniel did not realize God was sending help, but that the help had been delayed in coming. He continued to fast and pray for three weeks.

Stewart kept on praying, too. God sent the answer he needed when the time was right. Only God knows the best timing for answered prayers. Some have prayed for years, seemingly without an answer. But God hears and He will send the answer to that prayer.

The answer is often not what we expect, but God always knows the best way to answer. If our prayer is not in His will, He might say "No". He might say "Not now". God will answer the prayers of His children.

****

THE MERRY-GO-ROUND

Mary sank into bed finally about 1:00 am. *What an unbelievable week* she thought. She knew sleep would elude her. Her mind was racing with all the problems that occurred in the last three days.

Car problems started this merry-go-round Wednesday night and she had to miss church. Her sister in the hospital was not doing well. Job obligations were especially complicated and heavy and had to be completed before Monday morning. Now her rebellious daughter was coming in hours past curfew and not even contrite at all.

It seemed the phone never stopped ringing with more problems. Even the roof began to leak in the heavy rain today. She certainly didn't have enough savings for a new roof. What next?

Mary was desperate! She didn't know which problem to tackle first. Thank God, tomorrow was Sunday. With that thought, she fell into an exhausted sleep.

Her daughter apologized for her attitude and lateness as they got ready for church the next morning. Mary called the hospital and her sister was better. Entering the church, Mary spoke to friends who had their own roofing business. They agreed to either repair or install a new roof with payments to meet her budget.

With great relief, Mary sat in the familiar pew. The service began with a comforting chorus about coming into His house and worshiping Him. Mary felt surrounded by the peaceful atmosphere.

Pastor started his message with the words, "Let's stop the merry-go-round." She felt like he was speaking directly to her. He mentioned all the pressures of life that seem to be getting heavier all the time.

By the end of the service, Mary was strengthened and no longer desperate with pressures. She knew she would never have to go through these things alone. Resting and gaining strength in the Lord's house, she would face the next week with confidence that the problems would not rule her life.

Hebrews 10:25 Not forsaking the assembling of ourselves together, as the manner of some is; but exhorting one another: and so much the more, as ye see the day approaching.

~~~~~~~

The Sabbath day was made for Christians to be helped along in their journey. It is a time to worship God, a time to be comforted, a time to be strengthened and a time to be refreshed.

Fellow Christians try to help others. The music is uplifting. The message is usually just what is needed. It's very important for the followers of Christ to attend the church services regularly.

****

EMBEZZLEMENT

"Jerry I just can't figure it out," Glenda tossed the ledger onto the desk in frustration. "We have so many more contracts and you're putting in 16-hour days, yet we can barely meet expenses."

"I know, Glenda. It doesn't make any sense. This week we can't even meet the payroll. We'll have to skip our own salaries again. Eric works so hard keeping the books, and he can't explain it either. Everything looks good and appears to balance yet somehow there is never enough money to make any profit."

Glenda picked up the book again and opened it. "I know that somewhere there is a drain, a mistake or something wrong. I'm going to find it if it takes all night. You get some rest. First I'm going to pray for God's help and then, with a fresh pot of coffee, I'm going to dig in again."

About 3:30 that next morning, Glenda's attention was drawn to what appeared to be a normal listing in the ledger. It just wasn't quite right. In shock she realized what had happened. It was just fancy twisting and turning of the figures in the ledger. Over and over she found the same thing and in amazement she realized that the trusted bookkeeper was not to be trusted after all.

The next day, the Coopers signed a warrant and brought charges against the bookkeeper. Unfortunately, the missing funds could not be recovered.

Glenda faced the worst desperation of their lives as they lost their business. All the equipment had to be sold to recover from the huge debt which was much worse than they first realized.

In the coming weeks, they both found good employment with a solid company. Within the next two years, the area experienced a devastating economic slump.

The Coopers' business would have failed in that slump. They realized what a blessing it was to be back on their feet with stable employment when so many were out of work.

With the new jobs also came good medical insurance, something they had lacked as business owners. This was truly wonderful when their son suffered several broken bones and injuries in a bad accident. He had a very long and expensive recovery time.

Romans 8:31 What shall we then say to these things? If God be for us, who can be against us?

~~~~~~~

We often go through very hard times. Sometimes the things that we are going through are all part of God's plan for our lives.

He does see the end from the beginning and He knows just what we will be facing down the road. How wonderful to live knowing that He controls everything and will provide and care for us regardless of the circumstances.

****

9

BATTLEFIELD OF COMPLETE TRUST

SUDDEN DISASTER

The distraught woman rushed into the ER and to the first desk she saw. "Please help me, my husband, my daughter, someone called and said they were bringing them here. They had a wreck."

With uncontrolled tears flowing, she said, "Their name is Myers."

"Yes, Mrs. Myers, please have a seat over there and the doctor will be out to talk to you soon. I'll tell them you're here."

She sank into the seat in the corner of the room. Her eyes were glued to the door where the doctor might appear. She tried to pray, but nothing but the word 'Jesus' would enter her mind. Her focus was on the swinging door.

"Here." She rose and motioned to the tall, older man in scrubs as he came through the door and asked, "Myers?"

"Mrs. Myers, I wish I had better news for you. There was an explosion after the wreck. Your husband has severe burns and will need extensive treatment to survive.

Your daughter's burns are even more severe. I'm sorry to tell you that she possibly might not survive. She is getting the best of care and we are doing everything we can do. We'll keep you updated."

~~~~~~~

Ezekiel 37:3 And he said unto me, Son of man, can these bones live? And I answered, O Lord GOD, thou knowest.

God knows the end from the beginning. When our world comes crashing down, He is still in control. We might not have any idea of the outcome, but it helps to know that He knows exactly what is happening and what will happen in the future.

He wants us to trust Him and understand that He is in control. We want to focus on what man can do, but God is the one who holds the future in His hands.

He uses man to accomplish what He wants to happen. Whether it's good or bad, in our opinion, we have to trust that He knows why good and bad things happen and He knows what is best. One day perhaps He will let us know what and why these things happened. For now we have to trust Him.

****

RISING WATER

A flood is a devastating thing. The day was beautiful - warm with a slight breeze. The current was rushing and loud in the river, but by the house the waters were silently creeping, filling the low spots. Now it was on three sides of the house. The dark wetness was coming from across the road where the swamp was already full.

Audrey quietly watched, noticing the pump house was already surrounded. Down at the river, huge logs were riding in the swift current like they were motorized and driven. The concrete pelican was no longer visible on the dock and the dock itself appeared to be much higher at one end. Probably the posts were being undermined by the rushing waters.

At noon, Audrey wearing her boots, took the yardstick and walked around the house, measuring and writing on her notepad at certain spots to check the rise of the water. She noticed water creeping into the carport; soon the house would be surrounded.

Looking around, she saw one landmark after another had disappeared into the dark waters. The floor of the walkway to the dock was not visible. Only part of the railing still stood a foot or two above the rising waters.

This was supposed to be the last day before the waters crested, but how high would they get?

Widowed now four years, she felt she couldn't evacuate because of the possible vandalism that always seemed to occur in disasters. She did have the boat ready if necessary and the car had been parked on higher ground.

Even before her husband's death, they had never experienced flood waters like this. He made sure the home was built up four extra feet from the highest water they had heard of. But now, alone in this silence and surrounded by the black muddy waters, she wondered.

She had felt no fear, but now, doubt wanted to come into her mind. Grabbing her Bible, she knelt in the living room and asked, "Father, please don't let the water get in the house." Opening God's Word, He spoke to her through these words.

Isaiah 43:2 When thou passest through the waters, I will be with thee; <u>and through the rivers, they shall not overflow thee:</u> when thou walkest through the fire, thou shalt not be burned; neither shall the flame kindle upon thee.

The water did crest that day and begin to recede swiftly. Within a year, God impressed on Audrey's mind that it was time to sell that home and move. Two years later in another flood, the water did indeed flood the house belonging to the new owners.

****

THROUGH THE FIRE

"Cancer! No, it can't be. I've always been so healthy. Surely doc, you're not talking about radiation and chemotherapy and then maybe it still could come back?" Vance pondered these thoughts in his mind while waiting for the doctor to answer.

"Yes, Vance, that's exactly what could possibly happen, but we will do the best we know to do as doctors to cure this and prevent any recurrence. We know a lot more now than we used to. The treatments are not as evasive and devastating. The chance of recurrence is much smaller."

~~~~~~~

Daniel 3:25 He answered and said, Lo, I see four men loose, walking in the midst of the fire, and they have no hurt; and the form of the fourth is like the Son of God.

The king threw the three Hebrew boys into the furnace that had been heated up seven times hotter than normal. It was so hot, it killed the men who threw them into the fire.

The king looked into the furnace and he was shocked to see not three, but four men and they were all walking around without any harm. Their hair was not singed, the clothing not burnt. They didn't even smell of smoke. Who was that fourth man that walked around with them and kept them from burning in those flames?

Even the wicked king recognized the fourth man as the Son of God. He said there is no other God that can deliver like this.

In this life, there are hard times that we might have to endure and go through, but it's still the same as it was in the Bible. God can help us in our time of trouble. In the midst of our fiery furnace, God can walk with us and give us comfort and protect us from any damage the flames might have upon us.

If it's in His will that we succumb to that trial and not recover, then God alone can give us the comfort and peace needed to go through it.

When things are really bad, we might think we simply cannot take any more right now. Then we have to remember - He is in control, not us; trust, wait and obey.

****

ACCEPTING HIS WILL

For several weeks, the scripture *Matthew 28:19* had been burning in Breanna's heart. She couldn't get it out of her mind. It was about going out to all the nations and teaching and baptizing them.

"Do you think God is calling me to the mission field?" she questioned her father nervously. "I've never really even felt God's call at all. Why would He call me now? The only work I've ever done in the church was to help in the vacation Bible school; I'm not experienced in anything else.

I just got that good promotion at work. Of course what really concerns me is my marriage to Dave next May. I just couldn't agree to do anything without more details of what, where and when. All I can think about is that scripture."

"Well, Honey, first of all, whoever God calls, He qualifies, and He takes care of all the details. God does seem to be speaking to you. Sometimes He doesn't give us all the information we want. He requires obedience and trust. Let's continue to pray about what He wants you to do until He opens the door."

~~~~~~~

Daniel 12:8, 9 And I heard, but I understood not: then said I, O my Lord, what shall be the end of these things? And he said, Go thy way, Daniel: for the words are closed up and sealed till the time of the end.

Daniel didn't understand his vision. Like us, he wanted more information to clarify the vision in his mind. God said, 'No'! The words are closed and sealed until the end time.

So often we want to know, 'Why?' We want more details, more understanding. But God, who knows the end from the beginning, says it's not necessary to know any more right now. He is in control, not us; when the timing is right, He will reveal what we need to know. Maybe just one day at a time.

****

DON'T GIVE UP

The two friends sat on the back porch while enjoying their coffee. The day was beautiful. Their health was good but Dorrie knew her friend was depressed and saddened over something.

"OK, Anne, tell me what is bothering you; you've been depressed for several days."

"It's the children, Dorrie. I've prayed so long, over forty years now. But their hearts are cold and hard. It seems like the Lord's return is so close.

Will they ever get saved? I won't be around to pray for them much longer. Lately, I've wondered if there is any hope. All this time and their hearts are just like stone. I can't help but wonder sometimes if God hears my prayers."

"Oh, Anne, let me remind you of a story in the book of John. Remember the story of Lazarus? In John 11 it says that Jesus told them to roll away the stone. He said to Martha that all she needed to do was believe."

John 11:40, 41 Jesus saith unto her, Said I not unto thee, that, if thou wouldest believe, thou shouldest see the glory of God?
Then they took away the stone from the place where the dead was laid. And Jesus lifted up his eyes, and said, Father, I thank thee that thou hast heard me.

"Jesus told them to *take away the stone from the place where the dead was laid.* That certainly can apply to the spiritually dead as well as the physically dead. Notice also that He thanked the Father. It's so important that we give God thanks for all He does.

"When Jesus told Lazarus to come forth, he did!"

John 11:44   And he that was dead came forth, bound hand and foot with graveclothes: and his face was bound about with a napkin. Jesus saith unto them, Loose him, and let him go.

"Lazarus was bound in the grave clothes, just the way our loved ones are spiritually bound. When Jesus spoke, the binding was loosed. Remember there is no binding so tight that it cannot be broken when Jesus speaks."

~~~~~~~

Stony hearts can be moved and broken. It is not too late! Satan would lie and tell you "they'll never be saved," "it's too late," or "their hearts are too hard." That is a lie. God does hear our prayers, but there is a proper time for everything.

Remember, Jesus didn't go to the grave of Lazarus until three days after he was buried.

John 11:45 Then many of the Jews which came to Mary, and had seen the things which Jesus did, believed on him.

When it's the right time, everything will be perfect. Others will see and believe.

Your prayers will not go unanswered. We might never see that answer ourselves, but God does hear and He does answer when the time is right.

****

FORGETTING TO TRUST

It was late afternoon when Sara returned home that Christmas afternoon. All was quiet when she got out of the car, except for a strange sound of water pouring out from under the utility building door.

It had been four months now since that unwanted word 'widow' had become a reality. Now it was Christmas, a very cold one with snow and ice which was so unusual in North Florida. Today it had warmed up, but it felt so very depressing for this lonely woman.

Christmas has always been such a happy family time. Cooking the big dinner and having the family home. Trent always loved the family time and the holiday meals. She couldn't face it this year. Instead the family went out to eat. Later, Sara visited the nursing home.

Staring at the water, pouring out from under that door, she remembered the water pipes to the old washing machine, unused for years. She forgot to protect those pipes against the hardest freeze they had ever had. Now the pipes had burst and with the thawing, there was water everywhere.

All the difficult problems of the last four months seemed to culminate in this final Christmas Day crisis. It was just too much. Angry tears poured down her face. The crushing weight of widowhood was unbearable at that moment. Why had he died? She was too young to be a widow. Why didn't he prepare her to handle things like this?

It was then she remembered the day after he died. It was that moment of panic when reality edged into the shock. She was on the verge of hysteria, 6000 miles from home and so many details to handle. What would she do?

That was the moment her precious Savior wrapped His loving arms around her and spoke to her heart. "Don't you trust me, my child?"

Those words came back that Christmas afternoon and she knew they would many times in the future. The plumbing was fixed by a kind neighbor. Her spirit was mended one more time and she again rested not in her own strength, but in the strength of Christ.

~~~~~~

Proverbs 3:5,6 Trust in the LORD with all thine heart; and lean not unto thine own understanding.
In all thy ways acknowledge him, and he shall direct thy paths.

Often when pressures of life build up and push in on us, we tend to forget the promises Christ has made to us. He will lovingly remind us of His love and care as we turn back to Him.

****

10

THE BATTLEFIELD OF FEAR

UNEXPECTED FEAR

When Linda heard the tap at the door, she was sure it was the maintenance man coming to fix the closet. The retirement building had a good security system.

Guests called the residents from downstairs to announce themselves before they entered the lobby. This let her always know when someone was coming up to her apartment. If anyone else knocked, she knew it was a friend in the building or the people who worked there.

She opened the door to see the shocking situation of six uniformed policemen standing in the hallway. Her mouth fell open as they asked her to please step out. They surrounded her and walked her to the bench by the elevators.

They assured her she would be fine and asked her to please remain on the bench while they looked in her apartment. Then they proceeded to escort all the other people from their rooms, down to the area where Linda waited. All were out except the ninety-year old man across the hall from Linda.

They were then asked to go downstairs and wait in the recreation room until they called them.

It was a long wait! Linda was calm, as she knew the peace and tranquility of knowing Christ. Many of the other residents were upset, almost hysterical in not knowing what was going on or why.

Mrs. Walker wailed, "I'm so afraid! What are we going to do? Why are there policeman everywhere in our quiet building?"

Linda tried hard to comfort those that were upset. "I'm sure it will be over soon. It's probably nothing at all."

The worried group anxiously watched out the window as more policeman and members of the S.W.A.T.

team arrived and went upstairs. During the next hour, the people became more and more agitated and anxious.

Linda grabbed a Bible from one of the tables and began to read aloud the most comforting Psalm she knew.

Psalm 23:1-6   A Psalm of David. The LORD is my shepherd; I shall not want.

He maketh me to lie down in green pastures: he leadeth me beside the still waters.

He restoreth my soul: he leadeth me in the paths of righteousness for his name's sake.

Yea, though I walk through the valley of the shadow of death, I will fear no evil: for thou art with me; thy rod and thy staff they comfort me.

Thou preparest a table before me in the presence of mine enemies: thou anointest my head with oil; my cup runneth over.

Surely goodness and mercy shall follow me all the days of my life: and I will dwell in the house of the LORD for ever.

"Who else has a comforting scripture they'd like to read?" Several others responded with their favorites and the group was much calmer when the policeman arrived in the room to assure them that all was OK and they could return to their rooms.

It seems the elderly gentleman who lived across the hall from Linda, decided he was threatened by someone and he strapped on a holster with a handgun and walked through the halls and downstairs.

The staff called the police to avert a tragedy. Of course after reasoning with him, which took some time, he surrendered the handgun to the officers.

~~~~~~

We don't always know what and why things are happening around us. In those situations, we must remain calm and help to do whatever we can to help others.

Linda proved to be a faithful child of God in comforting the others around her. She also remained calm herself, although it was a difficult and stressful time.

****

STORMS

As Bonnie knelt to pray, a severe thunderstorm raged outside. She remembered a time many years before, when she had been so fearful of storms, the fear had almost paralyzed her.

Her boys were very small, her husband stationed overseas. She and her two sons lived in a mobile home in an area where thunderstorms were common most of the year.

Although she wasn't a Christian, she remembered several occasions during bad storms, taking the boys into the hallway, and kneeling and praying for protection. She didn't realize that while God always hears and answers the prayers of those who are saved, God might not answer the prayers of those who are not His children.

Years later, after she asked Jesus into her heart, she remembered a day in the car. Bonnie was on her way home from work in the middle of a violent storm. She felt a little frustration because she knew it would delay her reaching home.

Suddenly, Bonnie realized she felt absolutely no fear at all. She had no idea when God had delivered her from that fear, but it was completely gone. Even with the violent crashing of the thunder all around her, the heavy wind and rain falling, her heart and mind were filled with incomprehensible peace.

She still respected the fact that damage could be done and to be extra careful with her driving, but the tormenting fear was gone.

Now, years later in her living room, as she prayed, she began her time with the Lord, thanking Him again out of a grateful heart for deliverance from that dreadful fear.

~~~~~~~

2 Timothy 1:7 For God hath not given us the spirit of fear; but of power, and of love, and of a sound mind.

The child of God has been given a peaceful mind to face all the situations they might need to face. Before a person is saved, their mind is subject to many fears and torments. After salvation, just the knowledge that God is in complete control of everything gives an unfathomable peace to every situation.

1 John 4:18 There is no fear in love; but perfect love casteth out fear: because fear hath torment. He that feareth is not made perfect in love

Philippians 4:6,7 Be careful for nothing; but in every thing by prayer and supplication with thanksgiving let your requests be made known unto God. And the peace of God, which passeth all understanding, shall keep your hearts and minds through Christ Jesus.

Satan would love to torment the Christian with fear. The answer is simply to stay close to God. Read the Word, stay close to Him in prayer and give thanks for what He has done in the past. We are more than conquerors and overcomers through our faith in Christ.

****

ALONE WITHOUT GOD

They were in the hills of a turbulent Middle Eastern country. In that desolate area, there were many groups of enemy insurgents. They had attacked and set land mines to blow up the supply convoys.

Brad's squad had parachuted into the hills, under cover of the dark night, to search out and find the enemy and destroy them.

They knew it was a dangerous mission, but they had all volunteered to go. Quietly, they searched the hill where the enemy was supposed to be found.

Suddenly, bursts of mortar fire seemed to come from several directions. Four of the five troopers were hit, including the one with the radio that could summon help.

Brad found cover in a small cave that he accidentally stumbled into. He knew there was no way out of the situation and sooner or later they would find him.

Zephaniah 1:6 And them that are turned back from the LORD; and those that have not sought the LORD, nor enquired for him.

Brad thought of his parents and his two-year-old son. He also thought about the life he had wasted with drinking and constant partying. He loved the military and somehow kept his private life separate from the strict, regulated life in the service.

He wondered what would have happened if he hadn't turned away from God and joined the hard-drinking group. He had been a strong leader in the young adult group at church and wanted to dedicate his life to serving God.

But then he fell in with a wild group of friends. Would his wife have left him? Would he be alone and isolated now with no place to turn? He wondered if it was too late to turn back to God. To at least make peace with Him before the inevitable happened.

"Oh, God, I'm so sorry," he prayed. "Please forgive me. Let my parents and my wife know that I'm sorry for all the hurt that I've brought them. I'm afraid to die without you in my life. Please forgive me and save me. I don't believe there is a way out of this situation but thank you for hearing my prayer and giving me peace before I die."

Then, Brad heard the sound of helicopters. Unbelievably they had come to rescue him. The communications trooper had been able to get the message out before he died.

Isaiah 59:1 Behold, the LORD'S hand is not shortened, that it cannot save; neither his ear heavy, that it cannot hear:

~~~~~~~

It's never too late to call upon the Lord to save you in your time of trouble. He is faithful and just to hear our requests and He knows the sincerity of our hearts. Some stray and turn back from the Lord but He will hear us when we call and come back to Him.

****

FACING THE FEAR

Lynn took a deep breath and slowly exhaled. She watched the face of her daughter who had finally fallen into a troubled sleep. Lynn hoped it would be quiet in the hospital and Tracey could get some rest for a few hours.

Fear seemed to permeate the room. *What if he didn't make it?*. Lynn silently prayed, *Father, I know you are with us even now, I refuse to give in to terror or panic because I know everything is going according to your perfect plan.*

Less than an hour ago they had rushed the baby by helicopter to the neonatal unit in Atlanta. There were no facilities to care for him here. He was 10 weeks premature and so tiny with so many problems. His dad, along with the pastor and others were driving the three hour trip to get there and be with him.

Tracey was too ill to go yet. Perhaps they would release her in another day or two. "Oh, Mom, I'm so afraid for him. He had tubes everywhere and he is so small. They didn't give us much hope." Tracey sobbed, unable to sleep more than a few minutes.

"Tracey, I know what you are feeling, but we must not give in to fear. We must pray and place little Levi in the Lord's hands completely. If the Lord will spare him and heal his little body, we will dedicate ourselves to being Godly examples for him. We will raise him to love the Lord with all his heart.

Children are a gift from God, given to us to raise and bring up to love Him. Sometimes for His own reasons, He calls us home sooner than others would want. No matter what happens, we must commit this child to the Lord for His care and promise. If He heals Levi, we will need to bring him up to know and love God."

James 5:14,15 Is any sick among you? let him call for the elders of the church; and let them pray over him, anointing him with oil in the name of the Lord: And the prayer of faith shall save the sick, and the Lord shall raise him up; and if he have committed sins, they shall be forgiven him.

~~~~~~~~

Seventeen years later, Levi was strong and healthy. He loved God with all his heart and planned to dedicate his life to Him.

He was very different from most teenagers. He spent much time in prayer and reading God's Word. He witnessed to others and had already begun to teach and minister to others.

Lynn would always believe that because of the commitment that was made in that hospital room, God placed a strong calling on Levi's life and he would devote his life to the Father.

****

BILLS

"I just don't know what to do, Barbara, we are being wiped out by these huge medical bills. I can't let Ben know how bad it is. He's got enough to worry about. The fear about what will happen in the future is really bad.

I don't know how much longer he can work with his medical condition. Without his insurance, my medical insurance really isn't sufficient to handle all of his needed care. His insurance is good right now, but it doesn't cover the cost of all the medicine. It probably will soon reach the lifetime maximum the company allows."

"Sandy, sometimes we're just too close to the situation to realize that God always takes care of the future. In fact, He knew the future from the very beginning of this. He doesn't reveal it to us for a very important reason which is the need to trust Him!"

"You are so right, Barbara. I think Satan invented bills just to torment our minds. Isn't it true that for medical bills, as long as we pay something every month, it shows good faith and good intentions and maybe they will let us continue to pay that way?"

"Well, that's what we had to do after my heart attack. After a while, some of the bills were actually reduced and forgiven. It probably doesn't always happen like that, but we do what we have to do. I'm pretty sure that the church has a benevolent fund for emergencies too. Why don't you check into that?"

Romans 8:28 And we know that all things work together for good to them that love God, to them who are the called according to his purpose.

Having trust in those fearful times can be difficult. Trust and reliance that God will bring those things to pass that He intended to happen. All things happen for a reason. We must trust Him. The psalmist wrote that the righteous are not forsaken.

Psalm 37:25 I have been young, and now am old; yet have I not seen the righteous forsaken, nor his seed begging bread.

****

11

THE BATTLEFIELD OF FACING THE DARKNESS

ACCEPTING THE UNKNOWN

"No, Mrs. Graham, we're not sure exactly where the plane went down, yet. But it did crash. It completely disappeared off of the radar and we still don't know why.

The water is much too deep to ever recover the black box. Since it's in the middle of the Pacific, we most probably will never recover any of the bodies. I'm sorry." The tall captain, along with the Air Force Chaplin, related the sad news to Myra Graham and her daughters.

After the officers left, Myra sobbed to her pastor. "How can I face this? Not knowing any details of what where or why, not even having a body to bury. How can we even have a funeral service?"

Her pastor gently spoke, "Myra, we don't know any details but God does; that's really all that matters. We do know that Frank is in a much better place than we are right now. He was a very strong Christian and he will be waiting for us when we get to Heaven."

"I know you're right," Myra answered. "But, if only I could see him once more, tell him how much I love him. If we could just have the closure of having his remains to bury, I think I could accept it better. He was my youngest child and it's so hard to accept."

Isaiah 40:31 But they that wait upon the LORD shall renew their strength; they shall mount up with wings as eagles; they shall run, and not be weary; and they shall walk, and not faint.

Mark 13:27 And then shall he send his angels, and shall gather together his elect from the four winds, from the uttermost part of the earth to the uttermost part of heaven.

In the midst of tragedy, we sometimes cannot see any way that we will ever recover, or any way that we can get through the days that will follow. God always makes a way. He always gives strength to those that will lean on Him.

Even if man cannot find the remains of those that lose their lives they are not lost to God. Nothing is too hard for Him. He will gather those remains. Not to return them to a funeral home on this earth, but to take them to that Heavenly home, just as His Word promises.

****

WARNING SOUND

Shari walked quickly in the pre-dawn darkness of that January morning. It was a familiar route to her and the darkness didn't hinder her movements. It was cold as she dropped the trash in the container and walked briskly towards the paper box to get the morning paper. Suddenly, a deep warning growl sounded ahead of her towards the neighbors' trash cans.

Shari froze and quickly began a backward retreat, trying to see in the dim light what was threatening her. The neighborhood dogs behind their fences began with loud barking when they heard the growl. She knew bear sightings were very common in her area, but had never seen one near her house.

She exhaled a prayer of thanks when she shut the front door behind her, and decided to wait for the daylight in the future to venture towards the street.

An hour later, in the daylight, she cautiously walked toward the paper box, and saw the neighbor's trash completely demolished over a wide area.

Distinctive bear tracks were obvious in the mud at the side of the road. Shari thanked God for His protecting hand and knew she would use more wisdom in the future.

~~~~~~

1Thessalonians 5:5 Ye are all the children of light, and the children of the day: we are not of the night, nor of darkness.

Christians need to see where they are going. They are children of light and not children of darkness. There are a lot of things that scurry around in the darkness and hide when the light comes on. They hate the light and love the security of the darkness. Things of the darkness have no appeal to a child of the light. Certain things in the darkness need to be avoided.

This world is full of dark and evil things. These things should hold no interest for a Christian. They all don't give out a growl of warning. Christians must make sure they don't associate with the things of the darkness. The closer they stay to the Light of God, the more they will avoid dark things.

To be a child of light means that others can see Christ, in whom there is no darkness at all in their lives. It means they belong to Christ and want to be like Him. One day they will go to that eternal city of light and live forever where all darkness is dissipated.

John 12:35, 36 Then Jesus said unto them, Yet a little while is the light with you. Walk while ye have the light, lest darkness come upon you: for he that walketh in darkness knoweth not whither he goeth.
While ye have light, believe in the light, that ye may be the children of light. These things spake Jesus, and departed, and did hide himself from them.

****

THE ENEMY ATTACKS

"I just can't believe how hard it is to get this Sunday school lesson together," moaned Gloria. "I really thought things would get easier once I agreed to do some work for the Lord. Now it seems that everything is so much harder. So many interruptions constantly keep me from studying and praying about the lesson."

"Well, get used to it, Gloria. I know that's not what you want to hear, but the enemy would do anything to keep your sixth-graders from having a good lesson on Sunday," answered Mary, a seasoned teacher.

"Remember what Pastor says about fighting a battle and being a good soldier? Well, this is what he's talking about. When you step out and go to work for Christ, Satan starts fighting."

"You've been teaching for years, Mary. How do you fight back and get those lessons together?"

"You've heard the term 'press in'? Well that's what I try to do. I guard my mind to keep Satan from getting a foothold. Put away every distraction, and pray and read God's Word. Think about things that are of God and not things just concerning this world," Mary answered.

~~~~~~

Ephesians 6:10-18 Finally, my brethren, be strong in the Lord, and in the power of his might.
Put on the whole armour of God, that ye may be able to stand against the wiles of the devil.
For we wrestle not against flesh and blood, but against principalities, against powers, against the rulers of the darkness of this world, against spiritual wickedness in high places.

Wherefore take unto you the whole armour of God that ye may be able to withstand in the evil day, and having done all, to stand.
Stand therefore, having your loins girt about with truth, and having on the breastplate of righteousness;
And your feet shod with the preparation of the gospel of peace;
Above all, taking the shield of faith, wherewith ye shall be able to quench all the fiery darts of the wicked.
And take the helmet of salvation, and the sword of the Spirit, which is the word of God:
Praying always with all prayer and supplication in the Spirit, and watching thereunto with all perseverance and supplication for all saints;

Christians are engaged in a spiritual warfare with Satan. This is a battle that will continue until we enter into that Heavenly home to come.

It's a battlefield of darkness, because Satan is a deceitful enemy and does not fight fairly. He often uses distractions or other hindrances to keep the Christian from accomplishing work for Christ.

When we recognize where these attacks are coming from, we can take the upper hand. Jesus told Satan to "get behind Him." We can do the same. We have weapons that are given to us and we must know how to use them.

We can begin the fight on our knees, because all great spiritual warriors kneel and pray to begin their fight.

****

VICTORY OR COMPROMISE

The static sound of the radio brought the senator's speech into the tent over the generator noise. The soldiers listened carefully to his plan to end the war quickly.

It included sitting at conference, and negotiating a plan where each side would have to make major concessions. There would not be a clear victory for either side. The troops would be withdrawn very quickly.

"Well, Rob, we could be going home soon if his plan goes through, but it sure does leave a bitter taste in your mouth that our country fought for nothing," Eddie shook his head.

"That's true, Eddie, that's exactly what it would mean. The senator is a diplomat. He's not in the trenches the way we are. He doesn't see the day-in and day-out accomplishments that have been made.

He also doesn't understand that a true victory would mean so much to these people. They would never have to live under that dictatorship again. That's what would creep back in if we pull out without a victory. A compromise is a death sentence to these poor people," answered Rob.

"I guess that speech really sounds good to most people who don't bother to learn the truth. That's the difference between a soldier and a diplomat, victory or compromise.

I wish they would listen to those of us who have lived here for months. Compromise is supposed to work for the good of all, but it never does. It's just giving in and trying to make it look okay. The evil is just too strong. I think the senator is just trying to build a name by his accomplishments. He'll be running for president next."

Romans 12:2 And be not conformed to this world: but be ye transformed by the renewing of your mind, that ye may prove what is that good, and acceptable, and perfect, will of God.

Colossians 2:8 Beware lest any man spoil you through philosophy and vain deceit, after the tradition of men, after the rudiments of the world, and not after Christ.

~~~~~~~

Compromise sometimes sounds so good. It means there is no clear victory over those things that hinder us, but just giving in a little here and there won't really matter. Before we know it, the little compromises we made and that sounded so good, have turned around and completely changed into something else.

A good soldier will fight for what is right. Not giving in to things that sound good and will end the fight temporarily. In the long run, being a soldier instead of a diplomat will win the victory and not just cause a temporary peace.

****

DOUBT

Oh no, that's the same log I stepped over thirty minutes ago. I'm going in a circle. I've got to accept the fact that I'm lost in these woods. It's almost dark now and no one even knew I was going hunting. There is no hope of anyone even looking for me until morning. Paul sat down on the rotted log and dejectedly covered his face with his hands.

Earlier, after having an argument with Ginny his wife, he decided to drive to the river and go downriver to an area where he hadn't gone hunting before. He went quite a ways, following the curvy river to find a likely spot, before tying up the boat.

Then somehow, he got turned around when the sky became overcast and he lost his direction. He had hunted in this general area along the river for years and had never been lost. But today he was distracted and just didn't mark his trail the way he should have. He hadn't carried a compass and his matches were in the boat.

I guess they'll figure it out when they see the boat and my gun is missing. No one would ever dream that I could get lost in the woods. They'll just be looking for my body knowing what a bad heart I have. I doubt if I can make it through the night. It's going to rain and turn colder in the next few hours.

Paul pulled Spanish moss down from the big oak tree he was sitting under and tried to cover up with it, but he really didn't have much hope. Already he began to feel that familiar tightness in his chest. His five 'o clock medicine was overdue.

The night sounds of the swamp were beginning. The swamp was teeming with wildlife. He knew there were alligators, as well as bobcats and wild hogs along with an occasional panther and bear in this area. Snakes also were a threat. He felt more hopeless than he had ever felt in his life.

When a loud scream sounded close by, Paul griped his gun. How could he even see to shoot anything in this blackness? He felt sure if they found him at all, it would be too late. Large drops of rain spattered on the leaves and his head. He began to shiver with the cold.

In the lonely hours, Paul began to pray. "Forgive me Lord, for losing my confidence in you. Lord, please restore my hope and take away this doubt that I will survive this night. Forgive me for failing you so many times. Please don't leave me alone. Even if it is my time to leave this earth, please take the fear and doubt away. In the name of Jesus, please hear me, Father."

Paul still huddled under the tree in the darkness; comforting peace filled his mind. He no longer felt alone and he no longer felt any doubt or worry.

He was still cold, still wet and still miserable. He knew that most of the fear had stemmed from doubt that entered his mind about making it through the night. Even the tightness in his chest seemed to go away as the rain ended.

Several hours later as the sky turned to gray, he prepared to make his way out of the swamp. He could hear boats on the river and knew they would find his boat soon. When he heard the voices calling, he answered and moved in that direction.

Luke 12:29 And seek not ye what ye shall eat, or what ye shall drink, neither be ye of doubtful mind.

~~~~~~~

Doubt is an ugly insidious thing. It robs us of peace. It starts as a simple thought then leads to fear and often panic. Doubt always includes uncertainty and hesitation.

Doubt, if unchecked, will consume a person with uncontrollable fear.

Matthew 14:31 And immediately Jesus stretched forth his hand, and caught him, and said unto him, O thou of little faith, wherefore didst thou doubt?

****

THE PARTY

"Oh come on, Missy. It's just pot. You know it won't hurt you. You wanted to come and be part of the most popular group, didn't you?

Let's go and get some vodka. Loosen up girl! You'll feel great in no time. This is a rocking party. Shawn got a hold of a good batch; crack in its prime form. Later on, we'll go upstairs and have even more wild fun."

Missy knew she had made a huge mistake and somehow she needed to get out of here and get a ride back home. She did want to belong to the popular group, but it just wasn't what she thought it was. Everything she believed and had been taught went against what was happening in this group. She knew she wanted no part of it.

Missy slipped out to the deserted front porch and speed-dialed her older brother's number.

"Mike, can you come and pick me up? It's really urgent. I'm at 5th and Harris, in front of the tan house."

"Sure, Missy, I'm on my way," her brother replied. "What's going on?"

"I'll tell you when you get here, I've just made a bad mistake and I've got to get out of here."

John 3:19-21 And this is the condemnation, that light is come into the world, and men loved darkness rather than light, because their deeds were evil.

For every one that doeth evil hateth the light, neither cometh to the light, lest his deeds should be reproved.

But he that doeth truth cometh to the light, that his deeds may be made manifest, that they are wrought in God.

~~~~~~~

People that love evil, love the darkness. They look for pleasure in sinful things like illegal drugs, alcohol or illicit sex. These are things that belong in the darkness and not in the light.

Those who are Christians will do just the opposite. They will love righteousness and things of the light and hate evil, dark things. They will be very aware that the evil things of the darkness are something to be avoided.

It's not enough for a Christian just to love the things of God; they have to hate those things that are not of Him.

Christ loved righteous things and hated that which was evil; at the same time had a great compassion for those whose lives were being destroyed by evil. In that, he set the example for all to follow.

Missy would spend many hours in prayer for this misled group of 'friends'. She would never attempt to join in their activities again. Her life would be a compelling witness for good and against evil.

****

12

THE BATTLEFIELD OF SPIRITUAL MATURITY

AIRBORNE

Dean Wilson's mind was busy as he drove home from the out-of-town hospital. He set the cruise control for the speed limit, and thought of the family he had been visiting with. They were so glad he made the effort to be with them as the wife faced surgery.

He turned his mind to that Wednesday-night message he would be sharing in just a few hours. It was cloudy and beginning to rain, which cut the visibility. Dean had confidence in his driving ability and didn't slow down.

He was distracted with other thoughts as he drove on the interstate. There was the regular heavy late-afternoon traffic and he hoped the rain wouldn't worsen.

Soon he approached the high, curved bridge above the large river. At the highest point of the bridge, because he was following too closely, the vehicle ahead of him blocked his vision of the object in the road. They had managed to straddle it but Dean just didn't see it in time. He violently struck it with his left front tire.

The SUV went airborne, sharply turning right. All control went out of Dean's hands as it sailed towards the four-foot guardrail above the river.

In that brief second, Dean implored, "Jesus, help!"

Amazingly, the car righted as it hit the highway, again heading in the right direction. Dean carefully drove the car with the split tire, to the foot of the bridge and pulled over. He was praising God for His care and miraculous protection.

The car behind him pulled over, too. The man jumped out almost hysterical with amazement.

"How did you avoid jumping that guard rail? I saw it. You were in the air, going over and then it just turned and came back to the road."

"Well, my friend," Dean answered shakily, "It's called the amazing protection of Jesus. I was going too fast for the conditions and my mind was distracted. I have to admit my heart stopped for a moment looking at the circumstances.

Apparently it isn't my time to leave this world. God just gave me a wonderful testimony to share with the people tonight. The confidence I had in my own skills has lessened. But my confidence in God and His abilities has increased. I better get the spare out and change this tire."

~~~~~~~

Matthew 28:18 And Jesus came and spake unto them, saying, All power is given unto me in heaven and in earth.

Matthew 28:20b...... lo, I am with you alway, even unto the end of the world.

Miracles are not too hard for our God. He specializes in them. He is always with us and we can count on Him to do whatever is necessary for our situation. He cares about us and he cares about those happenings in our lives.

We don't know how much harm the enemy tries to inflict on Christians. We do know he hates every child of God. He would love to kill or at least destroy them spiritually so they would not be effective in God's work.

A Christian should always rely on God. But he should also do what is prudent and necessary to live in a responsible way. There is a refining process that we all must constantly go through to keep us in the proper condition to be used.

We can count on our Lord to protect and keep us safe when we stay in His will. Even if we are hurt, or we die, we can rest assured God is in control of everything.

Thoughts from the Battlefield

If we never faced danger or death, our testimony would be stale and old and it wouldn't have a lot of meaning for others.

****

THE LESSON

435 BC

Joatham watched carefully as his father sat in front of the extremely hot fire with the silver.

"Papa, can I try it now?"

"No, Joatham, first you much watch. It's a difficult process, you see, and much observing is required before you try it yourself," his papa answered.

"First, the crushed metal has to be heated at a very high temperature to separate the silver from the other metals. But you can't leave it too long; it must be watched carefully by the refiner.

Then, we will pour it into the clay pots where the impurities will float to the top and stick to the edges. That's when the silver becomes lustrous and the refiner can see his image in it."

"Is it ready then, Papa, to make the candlesticks and bowls?"

"No," his papa answered. But it is ready to be beaten and flattened. It must be constantly shaped and reheated before it can be worked into usable silver. Then it will make a beautiful silver bowl.

Remember always, Joatham, it is much in the same way that the Master works with us so we can be used and reflect His image. "

Malachi 3:2,3 But who may abide the day of his coming? and who shall stand when he appeareth? for he is like a refiner's fire, and like fullers' soap:
And he shall sit as a refiner and purifier of silver: and he shall purify the sons of Levi, and purge them as gold

and silver, that they may offer unto the LORD an offering in righteousness.

Through many trials and tribulations, the rough edges of Christians are smoothed. The sharp places are rounded until we closely resemble our Savior.

We are often crushed, roasted and melted to separate things in our lives that shouldn't be there.

That forming-and-beating process is often painful. God reproves and corrects us only because He loves us the way a loving father does. He never intends to destroy us, but to purify us and make us stronger.

Malachi 3:4 Then shall the offering of Judah and Jerusalem be pleasant unto the LORD, as in the days of old, and as in former years.

Then the offering of our lives will be pure and pleasant unto the Lord. He will begin to see His reflection in us. We are meant to be more like Him and our lives should reflect Him. They should reflect enough so that others will see Him in us.

****

GUILT

Dianne squirmed on the pew. Why did she sit so close to the front? *I can't get up and leave now. It would be embarrassing and everyone would know I'm leaving because of the message,* she thought to herself.

Oh no, does Pastor know everything? Did he follow me around last week? I wish I hadn't come, or at least have sat further back. I suppose he's going to talk about watching those TV shows now. I knew I should have changed the channel.

Is he looking right at me or am I imagining it? Oh boy, here it comes, laziness. I knew better than to miss those two Sundays and Wednesdays. I just wanted to do other things and sleep late.

I've been so miserable. I knew I had to get back in church and now he's just making a public example of me. Everyone probably knows he's only preaching to me. Well, he's almost through. When he calls for prayer, I'll just slip out of the pew and head for the back. Nows the time; I'm going.........Oh no! Why did I go to the altar?

"Oh God, please forgive me, I'm guilty, please restore my soul," Dianne wept with uncontrolled sobs.

When Dianne arose from the altar some time later, she was amazed to see many people in the altar and many others kneeling in their pews. She had been so sure the message was only for her.

~~~~~~

Hebrews 12:6,7 For whom the Lord loveth he chasteneth, and scourgeth every son whom he receiveth.
If ye endure chastening, God dealeth with you as with sons; for what son is he whom the father chasteneth not?

God does deal individually with all of us. He loves us just like the loving Father He is. When we get out of His will, He will deal with us to bring us back where we need to be.

Sometimes He uses the pastor to bring a convicting message. Sometimes He uses His Word, and sometimes He just continues to convict our hearts, until we have to ask forgiveness for our lapses.

It's a beautiful cleansing thing to pray until we know God has received us back into His loving arms. Peace fills our hearts, instead of tormenting conviction.

****

INNOCENT?

"But, Marcie, you don't understand. It's all so totally innocent. When Beth moved out, I had to have a roommate quickly. The house payment is due next week and also the electric bill. I count on that income to help meet the bills.

Joe's a really nice guy. A Christian, too, I think. My boss recommended him, so I know he's OK. It's just completely harmless, Marcie; I really don't know why you're making such a big thing out of this." Joanne sat down on the sofa in frustration. "I've had male roommates before without any problems."

"Joanne, you weren't a Christian before. I know this is all new to you but let me just share a scripture and maybe you will see what I mean."

I Thessalonians 5:2 Abstain from all appearance of evil.

"I'm not saying that it's not innocent. I'm saying that it just doesn't look good. You are subjecting yourself to temptation," Marcie went on. "I know you're a new Christian and perhaps you just hadn't thought about how our witness is destroyed by the things we do. We have to consider what might look bad to someone else."

"Well I guess when I think about it, I really did have a kind of uneasy feeling, that it might not be quite right. You know, learning how to live the Christian life should come with a guidebook or something."

"Oh, Joanne, It does come with a guidebook! The Bible, which is God's Word directly to us, is our guidebook. The answer is always there if we just look for it. That's why reading His Word is just as important as praying and going to church to grow and mature as Christians."

"Joanne, I'd like to pray with you that God would send the roommate He wants you to have. Then I think you better call Joe before he gets all his stuff over here."

"Thanks, Marcie. You're a good friend to have and help me along the way."

~~~~~~~

It's very important that we mentor and help guide new Christians as they begin their new life. Many things seem normal and very acceptable in the world we live in. But are they normal and acceptable to God?

Marcie accepted Joanne's advice, but that's not always the case. Great care must be taken to speak the truth in love. A good friend will always be truthful and firm, basing their statements on God's Word.

****

I BELIEVE

It was lunchtime at Wilson Corporation and a group of six executives were sitting around the table in the break room. Jonathan Grant bowed his head and silently prayed before beginning to eat his meal.

"Jonathan, I notice that you always pray before your meal. Are you just superstitious or do you really claim to believe that stuff about Jesus and Him being a savior?" Don, the pushy office busy-body asked.

He went on, "Surely you don't believe that nonsense written about Him. All those things about the virgin birth, the miracles; how He died then rose from the dead. I just believe what I can see and prove for myself. Even if you believe those things, why do you always have to pray out in the open at lunch time?"

"Well, Don," Jonathan answered, "It's true that I didn't see those things, but I also didn't see the battle of Appomattox. I didn't see the flight of the Wright brothers, or the Pilgrims landing, either. Yet, I believe these things happened because of the historical writings and the resulting consequences.

I believe in Jesus, even though I didn't know firsthand of His virgin birth. I didn't see Him perform miracles. No, I didn't witness His death on the cross or when He arose from the dead. I also didn't see Him ascend into Heaven, but I know His Word is true and I believe it.

You see, when I repented and accepted Him, He changed me from a cynical, doubtful, unbelieving person, into one who trusts and believes.

He delivered me from life-consuming habits. He healed the pain in my body. He filled me with His Holy Spirit. He saved my crumbling marriage.

No, I haven't seen His life personally with my natural eyes, but I believe, based upon the evidence and the change in my life. I will always be so grateful for everything He has done in my life and that's why I thank Him for all things including the food He provides."

John 20:29 Jesus saith unto him, Thomas, because thou hast seen me, thou hast believed: blessed are they that have not seen, and yet have believed.

~~~~~~~

There will always be those who doubt and those who do not believe. Belief is centered on faith and faith is the necessary element to believe. Faith is how you respond to God's leading. Paul wrote that faith is: *"the substance of things hoped for and the evidence of things not seen." Hebrews 11:1*

Christians have a belief in things that they don't see and yet believe. They see the tangible results and that is enough. Even if there are no tangible results, faith and belief are still necessary. This is the only kind of faith acceptable to God that will triumph in the end. This kind of faith believes in God, accepts His Word as the infallible truth, and is obedient to the commands of God.

****

EPILOGUE

It is the nature of our lives to go through battles as we travel through the years. The Word of God tells us not to be surprised by this. The trials come to make us strong.

1 Peter 4:12 Beloved, think it not strange concerning the fiery trial which is to try you, as though some strange thing happened unto you.

We must not be unprepared for the battlefields and learn to endure like good soldiers. God normally does not take us out of the battlefield, but He walks with us through it.

He is able to take us out, but He may not. The three Hebrew boys, as they were going to be thrown into the fiery furnace, said they knew God was able to deliver them, but if He didn't, they still would not serve the heathen gods.

The Israelites fought many battles in the wilderness. They fought battles of sickness, heat, hunger and thirst. They had no comforts, no stores and no air conditioning. Even though they murmured against God, He loved and cared for them. He provided food, heat, shade, and clothing that never wore out.

He loves us, too, and will provide for us as we are strengthened in the midst of the battlefield. Sometimes He takes us out of the battle and sometimes He walks with us. We know He will never leave us there alone.

Thank you Lord, for going before us
Thank you Lord, for going behind us
Thank you Lord, for going with us

Thoughts from the Battlefield

Hebrews 13:5,6 ………..for he hath said, I will never leave thee, nor forsake thee. So that we may boldly say, The Lord is my helper, and I will not fear what man shall do unto me.

****

Authors Note

Battlefields are definitely not strangers to me.
During the writing of the book, I have faced numerous battlefields of my own.

While completing the final editing, an unlikely event led to one more physical confinement and this time to hospitalization.

Through it all, I recognize that God is still on the throne. He's never left my side. In the difficult times, He seems even closer. I give Him the praise and glory for being there during my personal battlefields.

Facing battles is part of life. It's how they are faced and who we depend on that makes the difference. To reach the end of this race, we have to fight through the battlefields. They make us strong, test our endurance and perseverance. Being prepared will affect the outcome.

This work is now going to print. The glory belongs to God!

Thoughts from the Battlefield

www.ingramcontent.com/pod-product-compliance
Lightning Source LLC
Chambersburg PA
CBHW032001040426
42448CB00006B/444